For Führer and Fatherland

POLITICAL & CIVIL AWARDS OF THE THIRD REICH

Hitler and members of his diplomatic entourage in Italy, May 1938.

and Fatherland

AWARDS OF THE THIRD REICH

BY
LTC
JOHN R.
ANGOLIA

2nd Edition

ISBN No. 0-912138-16-5

Copyright 1978
by
John R. Angolia
Second Printing--May 1989

Printed in the United States of America

Designed
by
Roger James Bender

Cover Design
by
Roger Waterman

Type set
by
Clyborne Typographics
and
Perez Productions

R. James Bender Publishing

P.O. Box 23456 • San Jose, CA 95153 • (408) 225-5777

Contents

Introduction

It is my pleasure to provide you with the second of two volumes dealing with the orders, decorations, medals and badges that were awarded or produced during the twelve volatile years of Hitler's Third Reich. Every effort has been made to provide all available, relevant information to preclude the necessity of yet another work. However, should sufficient information be forthcoming to warrant a third volume, I will make every effort to bring it to you.

Your first reaction may be one of disappointment that there is virtually no coverage dealing with reproductions, etc. It is my hope that the detailed study contained in the text, and the full scale representations, both front and back, of each award will provide you with sufficient information to allow you to make your own determination. The major problem in discussing reproductions is one of time and space. Reproductions in one form or another made their debut immediately after the conclusion of hostilities, and have undergone many changes over the years. Reproduction techniques continue to improve, and more and better copies are constantly being offered. Discussion on the matter would be largely overtaken by events before the book would become available. The single best advice I can give on the matter of reproductions is for you to become as knowledgeable as possible in your subject, to know your source, and when in doubt, to give way to your 'gut' feeling, as you are the one that ultimately has to be satisfied.

Certainly this work will stimulate an interest in presentation cases and award documents. Permit me a word of caution in this area. This material is starting to be reproduced as well, ranging from poor to near-perfect. There will be times when you will decide to turn down an available piece because it varies in some respect with the example shown in my works. You should understand that variations did exist during the period. These variations can be attributed to sub-contracting, changes in techniques, desired improvements, etc. For example, in every case where an award was open to foreign recipients, the award document was produced in two forms - one for the German national which bore the signature title 'Der Führer und Reichskanzler', and another for the non-German bearing the title 'Der Deutsche Reichskanzler'. Where I am aware of an original variation, I have made every effort to pass that information on to you. However, there are some variations of which I am not aware - this does not make them any less original. Simply exercise caution in this area in the same manner that you would when inspecting the award.

In most cases I have found that the original recipient values his award document far more than the award itself. This largely stems from the fact that it is proof positive that he received the award, and could have some bearing on a future pension. Of secondary concern is the signature found on the document; unless, of course, that signature should be signed by hand by someone like Hitler or an admired divisional commander. Presentation cases were then, and still are, viewed as nothing more than protective devices. A collector who is fortunate enough to obtain the original award in cased form along with the award document is very lucky, indeed, as these were usually separated over the years.

Acknowledgments

The list of willing contributors grows with each research project that I undertake. Each contributor should be proud of his contribution as he has had a hand in the finished product.

While my own collection and archives are rather extensive, I must continue to throw myself on the mercy of the collector and research historian in general to fill the gaps that continue to prevail. Those that are acknowledged here unselfishly responded to my call for help, and it is to them that this book is dedicated.

This work and others that are to follow would never have been completed had it not been for the technical assistance that was so freely given. I would like to express my sincere appreciation to Fräulein Inge Kettner for her long and tedious hours of translation of a myriad of regulations, articles and publications. A dear friend, John Hardey, has clearly demonstrated his ability with the camera, and has provided the photos so necessary in this work.

No degree of words can express the appreciation that I have for Bill Stump and the support that he has given me over the years on this and my previous works. A noted collector, Bill has spent years gathering material and making comparisons with the intent of doing a work of his own. He so kindly turned his material over to me for incorporation into my own research, and is content to see the information placed in the hands of the reader.

It is virtually impossible to establish an order of merit for the others who have given so freely of their time, knowledge and material. Below are but a few individuals and organizations that I would like to single out:

INSTITUTIONAL

Gary Walker Historical Museum
Imperial War Museum, London, England
Library of Congress, Washington, DC
National Archives, Washington, DC
Rastatt Army Museum, Rastatt, West Germany
US Military Academy Museum, West Point, NY

INDIVIDUALS

Verkuilen Ager
Kim Alstott
Ed Anderson
Doug Barton
Roger James Bender
Tom Bittner
Glenn Browning
B. Burke
Charles Campbell
Wm. Chizar
L. Clark
Gayle Dinsmore
Don Frailey
Christie Hannahs
Jeff Hanson
Bud Hasher
John Henigan
Bob Hritz
Jim Jones
Tim Knight
Bob Kraus

Dan Gleason
Russ Hamilton
Dan Leach
Ron Levin
Karen Kuykendall
MAJ George MacKlintock
Pete Malone
Bob McCarthy
Bill McClure
Wayne Milburn
Dr. Julian Milestone
Roland Oddera
Bob Odrobina
George Petersen
Jim Peterson
Bruce Regnemer
Ren Reynolds
George Robinson
Chuck Scaglione
Bob Stulga
Ben Swearingen

Frank Thayer
Gary Walker
Nuel Wallace
Ron Weinand
Jack Wells
Ray Zyla

FOREIGN CONTRIBUTORS

Chris Ailsby
Tom Bergroth
Eric Campion
Jean-Pierre Chantrain
Chris Farlowe
Rudolf Fetzer
Hartvig Fleege
Lothar Hartung
Dr. Kurt-Gerhard Klietmann
Leif Linde
Lt. Col. Maitland-Titterton
Dr. André Mathias

Andrew Mollo
Ernst Obermaier
Wm. Saris
Rene Smeets
O. Spronk
Fred Stephens
Alois Tress
Ludwig Umlauf
Fritz Walterman

and to those anonymous contributors who gave so much.

Author's Request

Once again I turn to the reader in search for support for future references that are currently being worked on. The works deal with the following subjects in probable order of publication:

1. From Bismarck to Hitler - German Military History from 1813 to 1945.

2. History of the Iron Cross and the Order of the Knight's Cross winners, possibly up to seven volumes.

I am in need of unpublished photographs of Knight's Cross bearers, information concerning their award that has not been published, and data concerning markings on the Knight's Cross and the various devices. If you have something you feel would contribute to any of these references, please send to:

LTC (Ret.) John R. Angolia
18070 Berryhill Dr.
Stilwell, KS 66085

Other books by the author:

"Swords of Hitler's Third Reich"

"Daggers, Bayonets and Fighting Knives of Hitler's Germany"

"Edged Weaponry of the Third Reich"

"Insignia of the Third Reich"

"For Führer and Fatherland--Military Awards of the Third Reich," Vol. I

"For Führer and Fatherland--Military Awards of the Third Reich," Vol. I, Revised

"For Führer and Fatherland--Political and Civil Awards of the Third Reich," Vol. II

"Belt Buckles and Brocades of the Third Reich"

"Cloth Insignia of the NSDAP and SA"

"Cloth Insignia of the SS"

"On the Field of Honor--A History of the Knight's Cross Bearers," Vol. I

"On the Field of Honor," Vol. II

"Uniforms and Traditions of the German Army, 1933-1945," Vol. I

"Uniforms and Traditions of the German Army," Vol. II

"Uniforms and Traditions of the German Army," Vol. III

"Swords of Germany, 1900-1945"

"The U.S. War Machine"

"The Pour le Mérite, and Germany's First Aces"

Constantin von Neurath

O. Spronk

Uational Awards

CROSS OF HONOR 1914-1918
(Ehrenkreuz 1914-1918)

On 13 July 1934 Reich President Generalfeldmarschall von Hindenburg instituted the Honor Cross of the World War 1914-1918 (Ehrenkreuz des Weltkrieges 1914-1918), thus giving rise to the unofficial designation of the 'Hindenburg Cross'. This award was the only official commemorative award issued during the Hitler era which recognized World War I service.

Three forms were established upon institution:

a. For Combatants (für Frontkämpfer): A bronze cross with the date '1914-1918' in the center surrounded by a laurel leaf wreath. Two crossed swords ran between the arms of the cross. The **reverse** of the cross was plain with the possible exception of the manufacturer's logo. The cross was worn suspended from a 30mm ribbon of black/white/black/red/black/white/black stripes.

b. For Non-Combatants (für andere Kriegsteilnehmer): Identical to a. above except that the **swords are omitted, and the wreath was of oakleaves.**

c. For Widows or Parents (für Witwen und Eltern): Identical to b. above, except that the cross was finished in black rather than bronze, and the suspension ribbon was white/black/white/red/white/black/white.

The design was the creation of Eugene Godet of Berlin, who had received specific directions from the Reich Chancellery. Each cross measured 38mm. However, a commercial version of the award for the widow or parents came into existence in pin-back form measuring only 31.5mm. It is not known if this brooch ever achieved official recognition.

By 1940 persons from the Saar, Danzig, Austria, Czechoslovakia and Memel who met the criteria for the award were also authorized to receive the Cross of Honor.

In an order signed by Hitler dated 17 December 1934, a battle streamer bearing the colors of the Cross of Honor ribbon was authorized to be affixed to the flags and standards of the Army and Navy.

By 1 February 1937 the following numbers of awards had been approved and rendered:

a. Combatant: 6,202,883
b. Non-Combatant: 1,120,449
c. Widow: 345,132
d. Parents: 373,950

For Combatants   **For Non-Combatants**

For Widows or Parents

This does not accurately reflect the total number of awards finally issued since eligibility was expanded with the acquisition of new territory. There may have been more Germans eligible who simply failed to apply for the award. Approving authority was vested in the Minister of the Interior.

The cross was presented with an award document. The manner of presentation varied - either the medal could be handed over in its basic form, come encased, or be presented in a binder having the award document on one side and the cross on the other. The Cross of Honor was accorded rather high recognition since it ranked above service and occupation awards, but below combat-related awards. The cross was worn on either a medal bar or in the form of a ribbon on a ribbon bar above the left breast pocket.

Leif Linde

Cross of Honor for Combatants in the original presentation case.   The exterior of the case was normally black, but also exists in red.   The outer portion of the lid bears no distinctive designation, while the interior has the dedication, "Treue um Treue", and a facsimile of Hindenburg's signature in black on white satin.   The lower section is off-white velvet, and is compartmented.

SS-Sturmbannführer Grimminger, bearer of the 'Blood Flag', is shown wearing the 1914-18 Cross of Honor on his medal bar.

Im Namen des Führers und Reichskanzlers

em

ist auf Grund der Verordnung vom 13. Juli 1934 zur Erinnerung an
den Weltkrieg 1914/1918 das von dem Reichspräsidenten Generalfeld=
marschall von Hindenburg gestiftete

Ehrenkreuz für Frontkämpfer

verliehen worden.

, den   19   .

Nr._____.

Award document for the 1914-1918 Cross of Honor (For Combatants)

Im Namen des Führers und Reichskanzlers

er

ist auf Grund der Verordnung vom 13. Juli 1934 zur Erinnerung an
den Weltkrieg 1914/1918 das von dem Reichspräsidenten Generalfeld=
marschall von Hindenburg gestiftete

Ehrenkreuz für Witwen

verliehen worden.

, den   193   .

Nr._____/3_.

Award Document for the 1914-1918 Cross of Honor (For Widows)

GERMAN OLYMPIC GAMES DECORATION
(Deutsches Olympiaehrenzeichen)

Preparations for the 11th Olympiad, to be held in Berlin, and the 4th Olympic Winter Games, to be held in Garmisch-Partenkirchen in February 1936, were placed in the hands of an able organizer, Reichssportführer SA-Obergruppenführer Hans von Tschammer und Osten.   In recognition of the considerable work that went into the Olympic Games, which were a Nazi showpiece, Hitler instituted the German Olympic Games decoration (Deutsches Olympiaehrenzeichen) in two classes on 4 February 1936.   It was to serve as an expression of gratitude from the German people through him.   Award of this decoration was extended to foreigners and to German nationals.   The two classes, designed by Professor Raemisch, were as follows:

a.   1st Class: A total of 767 1st Class awards were presented.   It was worn about the neck suspended from a 50mm neck ribbon of reddish-orange with five white stripes down the center and black edges.   The decoration, measuring 63mm at its widest point and 88mm high, was a combination of gold-plated bronze and white enamel.   The central motif was the five Olympic rings attached to the decoration by two rivets.   Presentation was made in a large white simulated leather case, and was accompanied by an award document personally signed by Hitler.

German Olympic Games Decoration 1st Class

It is not known what the '38' designation is.   Possibly it represents a serial number of the award.   Some awards were engraved on the back as well.

Note ribbon configuration for wear under a closed collar.

Presentation case for the German Olympic Games Decoration 1st Class. The case is white simulated leather with the five olympic rings embossed in gold on the lid. The inner portion of the lid is white satin, while the lower compartmented section is mouse-gray velvet.

In Anerkennung seiner Verdienste
um die Deutschland übertragenen

Olympischen Spiele 1936

verleihe ich dem

SS.-Brigadeführer Karl Wolff

das

Deutsche Olympia-Ehrenzeichen

erster Klasse.

Berlin, den *29. Oktober* 1936

Der Führer und Reichskanzler

Award document for the German Olympic Games Decoration 1st Class presented to Himmler's Chief-of-Staff, Karl Wolff.   The text is done in a combination of black and red colors.   Actual Hitler signature.

das

Deutsche Olympia-Ehrenzeichen

erster Klasse.

Berlin, den   1937

Der Deutsche Reichskanzler

Award document for the German Olympic Games Decoration 1st Class.   The signature block "Der Deutsche Reichskanzler" indicates that this document was intended for award to a non-German.

19

b.   2nd Class: This award was open to persons who played a significant, but lesser role, and 3,364 awards were bestowed.   It was worn on the medal bar above the left breast pocket.   When worn on the ribbon bar, a gold metal national emblem was affixed to it to distinguish it from the Olympic Games Commemorative Medal award.   It ranked below the service awards.   The design was basically the same as the 1st Class except that it was smaller (65mm at the highest point), and had a fixed ring rather than an elongated loop.   The ribbon was like the 1st Class, but measured 31mm.   It was also presented in a white simulated leather case along with an award document.   However, unlike the 1st Class document, the Hitler signature was only a facsimile.

Obverse

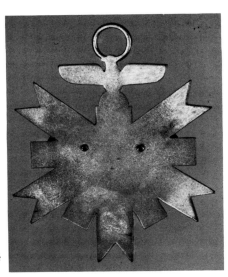

Reverse

German Olympic Games Decoration 2nd Class

The foundation decree prescribed that upon the death of the recipient the award would be turned over to the next-of-kin.

Recommendations for award were processed through the Minister of the Interior, with the award authority shared jointly by the Reich Chancellor and the representative of the Prussian state government.

20

In Anerkennung seiner Verdienste
um die Deutschland übertragenen
Olympischen Spiele 1936
verleihe ich dem

das
Deutsche Olympia-Ehrenzeichen
zweiter Klasse.

Berlin, den   1936

Der Führer und Reichskanzler

The signature block "Der Führer und Reichskanzler" indicates that the award of this German Olympic Games Decoration 2nd Class was intended for a German National.

General Oshima, Japanese Ambassador to Berlin, wears the Olympic Games Decoration 2nd Class on his medal bar.

OLYMPIC GAMES COMMEMORATIVE MEDAL
(Olympia-Erinnerungsmedaille)

54,915 persons received the Olympic Games Commemorative Medal (Olympia-Erinnerungsmedaille), which was instituted on 31 July 1936. The award was established to recognize services rendered in connection with the preparation and execution of the 11th Summer and 4th Winter Olympic Games held in Germany in 1936. It was in no way intended to be recognized as an award for participation, or placing in, an Olympic event. Award was not restricted to German nationals. However, persons who had received the Olympic games decoration 2nd or 1st Class were not eligible for this medal.

The silver medal, which measured 37mm, was suspended from a 31mm ribbon of reddish-orange with five white stripes down the center and black outer stripes. The obverse of the medal had a national emblem surmounting a column with five Olympic rings. The date '1936' was separated by the eagle and swastika. On the reverse was the inscription 'Für verdienstvolle Mitarbeit bei den Olympischen Spielen 1936' (For Meritorious Co-operation in the Olympic Games 1936), below which was a sprig of oak leaves.

The medal was authorized for wear either on the medal bar or in the form of a ribbon on the ribbon bar above the left breast pocket. It ranked below the service awards.

Obverse

Reverse

The presentation case for the Olympic Games Commemorative Medal is a white simulated leather hinged hard case. The outer lid has a gold outer edge and five Olympic rings in gold in the center. Inside of the lid is white satin. The lower portion is recessed to accept the medal, and is finished in gray velvet.

Jn Anerkennung ihrer verdienst-
vollen Mitarbeit bei den

Olympischen Spielen 1936

verleihe ich der

die

Deutsche Olympia-Erinnerungsmedaille

Berlin, den   1937

Der Führer und Reichskanzler

Award Document for the Olympic Games Commemorative Medal.

23

OLYMPIC VICTOR'S MEDAL
(Olympia-Siegermedaille)

With the advent of the 11th Olympiad, the German National Committee for Physical Training (Deutscher Reichsausschuss für Leibesübungen DRL) commissioned the design and production of the medallions to be awarded to the first three place victors. The medallions were produced in gold (1st Place), silver (2nd Place) and bronze (3rd Place). Award was made in a black presentation box before the cheering throngs in the Berlin Olympic Stadium. Two distinctive design medallions were produced for the Winter and Summer Olympic Games.

Obverse

Reverse

Preliminary events were held throughout Germany in an effort to find the best qualified person to represent Germany in the up-coming Olympic Games. Contests in all categories were held, and a team representing each particular sport was determined from the order of placement. Awards were rendered to the first three places. These awards were not officially connected with the Olympic Games, but should be considered as part of the preliminary award process.

Obverse

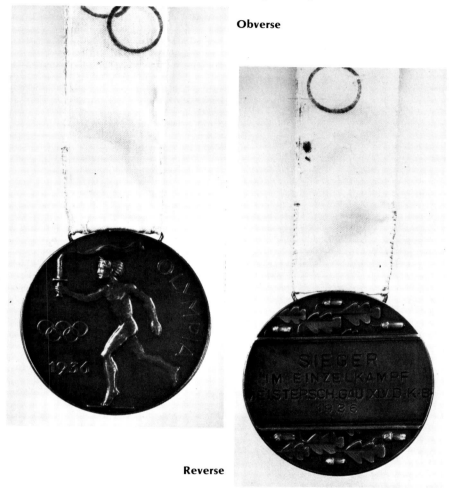

Reverse

Regional award presented to the 1st Place winner in the Master Class Shooting event. The medal is bronze suspended from a white ribbon bearing the five Olympiad rings.

Olympic Victor's Medal
or the Summer Games

Obverse

Reverse

1936 Olympic Medallion presented to all participants of the Olympic Games. The bronze medallion was designed by Otto Placzek. The medallion was presented in a black hard case with a burgundy velvet lower compartmented section.

GERMAN NATIONAL PRIZE FOR ART AND SCIENCE
(Ehrenzeichen des deutschen Nationalpreises für Kunst und Wissenschaft)

One of the rarest Nazi era awards, and certainly the most coveted of the national awards, was the German National Prize for Art and Science. Hitler personally instituted the award on 30 January 1937. He intended it to replace the Nobel Peace Prize since he had forbidden German citizens to accept the international award only one month earlier.

There was certainly good reason for the award to be coveted as much as it was. Besides having forty diamonds approximating ¼ karat each, the award also carried with it a cash sum of 100,000 Reich Marks. Albert Speer had this to say about the award, 'The decoration for which I had expressed my preference was the National Prize. It was thickly encrusted with diamonds and so heavy that the wearer had to have a pendant inside his dinner jacket to carry the weight.'[1]

The decoration, which was designed by Müller-Erfurt of Berlin, consisted of a breast 'star' measuring 96mm with gold stylized national emblems between each

Breast Star of the German National Prize for Art and Science

[1] *Albert Speer, Inside the Third Reich, New York: Avon, 1971.*

quadrant. Manufacturing variations were produced during the period. This is particularly evident in the design change in the national emblems between 1939 and 1943. In the center was the gold head of goddess Athene on a red enamel field encircled by the inscription 'Für Kunst und Wissenschaft' (For Art and Science). Around the outer edge of the inscription was a circle of 40 diamonds. The reverse of the star bore the silver content designation '935'. The badge, which was constructed in three layers, was held together by 14 rivets. In addition to the breast star there was a 105mm sash worn across the right shoulder and fastened at the left hip. The sash was

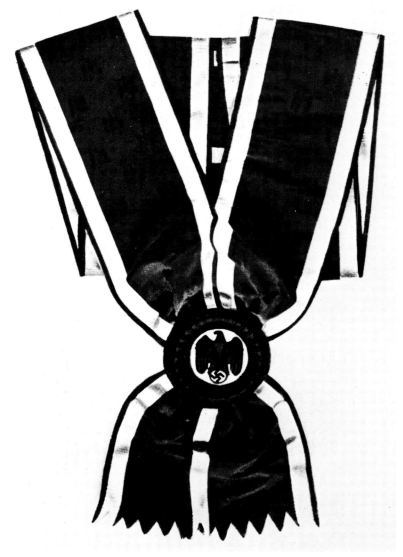

Shoulder sash and rosette portion of the prize. The shoulder sash measured 105mm. Note the national emblems woven into the red field.

ICH VERLEIHE HIERMIT

FERDINAND PORSCHE

DEN DEUTSCHEN NATIONALPREIS
FÜR KUNST UND WISSENSCHAFT

NÜRNBERG-DEN 6. SEPTEMBER 1938.

Document awarding the German National Prize for Arts and Science to Prof. Ferdinand Porsche. The award was rendered on 6 September 1938.

bright red with wide white stripes down each side, and small red outer stripes. Embroidered into the red field were red national emblems. Where the sash crossed the hip there was an 80mm rosette with a red national emblem with black swastika on a white enamel field encircled by a red border. This sash was worn on top of any other held by the recipient.

Prior to the introduction of the German Order in 1942, the National Prize was recognized as Germany's highest non-military award. It was first awarded on 7 September 1937 during the Rally at Nürnberg where the awards were made with great ceremony. The first award was symbolic in nature, and was presented posthumously to Hitler's personal architect, Professor Ludwig Troost, who had died three years earlier. Other awards for 1937, made at the same time, were bestowed upon:

a. Reichsleiter Alfred Rosenberg for his contribution to the Nazi movement.

b. Professor August Bier and Dr. Ferdinand Sauerbruch, who shared jointly in the cash award, but who both received the decoration. The joint award was made in recognition of their contributions to the field of medicine.

c. Professor Dr. Wilhelm Filchner, who was recognized for his explorations.

The following year's awards were also made on 7 September, and were presented to the following recipients:

a.   Dr. Fritz Todt, in recognition of his development of the German National road system or autobahn.

b.   Professor Dr. Ferdinand Porsche for his work in the development of the Volkswagen.[2]

c.   Professor Dr. Ernst Heinkel and Professor Willy Messerschmitt for their work in aircraft design and production.   Again, both men shared in the cash award, but both received the decoration.

In addition to receiving the award, the recipients were presented an elaborate award document.

While there is no record of further awards being made after 1938, possibly due to the outbreak of the war, the statement cited by Albert Speer earlier would indicate that as late as 1944 the award was still at least being considered.   It is possible that designations were made with the intention of making the actual presentation at the end of the war.

Reichsminister Dr. Goebbels congratulates the 1938 recipients of the National Prize.   From left to right: Dr. Goebbels, Dr. Heinkel, Prof. Messerschmitt, Prof. Dr. Porsche and Dr. Todt.

---

[2]*It should be noted that the award document rendered to Prof. Porsche is dated 6 September 1938.*

Hitler and Goebbels jointly present the National Prize for Art and Science award document to the second 1938 recipient, Prof. Messerschmitt.

NOTE:

Since there are only eight known recipients of
this award, this would rank the National Prize
before the German Order in degree of rarity.

MERITORIOUS ORDER OF THE GERMAN EAGLE
(Verdienstorden vom deutschen Adler)

After her defeat in 1918, Germany had no national order or decoration which could be bestowed upon foreign nationals. The bestowal of national awards to foreign dignitaries was extremely important, especially within the diplomatic arena, since the use of such awards was often the 'grease' that was applied to the rails of international progress. This situation was corrected on 1 May 1937 when Hitler instituted the "Meritorious Order of the German Eagle" (Verdienstorden vom deutschen Adler). Now Germany had an award that could be bestowed at the diplomatic level, and Hitler did not hesitate to take advantage of this. He was to use the order to curry favor among statesmen and well-known personages who visited Germany. He awarded it with an eye to the future, presenting it to those that might serve his cause at some future date. One notable American, Charles Lindbergh, accepted the award of the Meritorious Cross of the Order of the German Eagle with Star (Verdienstkreuz des Ordens vom Deutschenadler mit dem Stern) on 19 October 1938 from Hitler. After falling under the spell of Hitler and Göring, Lindbergh returned to the United States and tried to persuade the American people that they should favor Germany in her territorial claims if war was to be averted. Lindbergh was to have the company of many men of influence as Hitler selectively awarded Germany's new Order. One considerably less gullible recipient was Henry Ford.

The Meritorious Order of the German Eagle was initially intended to be awarded only to foreign statesmen and dignitaries, but this condition had changed by 1939. It was intended to rank with similar foreign awards - the equivalent of the American Legion of Merit, for example. Since the Order was to be an international one, it was graded along international lines, and accorded a relative order of merit. Bestowal was to be made according to the following international ranking system:

a. Knight (Ritter - low-ranking recipients not of officer grade): awarded the medal.

b. Officer (Offiziere): awarded the breast star.

c. Commander (Komture oder Kommandeure): awarded the neck order.

d. Grand Commander (Grosskomture oder Grossoffiziere): awarded the neck order and breast star.

e. Grand Gross (Grosskreuze): This award was bestowed in the form of a shoulder sash and breast star, and was usually reserved for award to heads of state, field marshals and others of notable rank.

The institution order of 1 May 1937 creating the Meritorious Order of the German Eagle established five Orders and one Medal of Merit as follows:

a. Grand Cross of the Order of the German Eagle (Grosskreuz des Ordens vom Deutschenadler). The original order gives the title of this award as "Grosskreuz des Ordens vom deutschen Adler", whereas the title on the award document is expressed as "Grosskreuz des Ordens vom Deutschenadler". It should be noted that the titles stated in the instituting order and those shown on the award documents coincide once the 1st degree award is reached.

b. Order of the German Eagle with Star (Verdienstkreuz des Ordens vom Deutschenadler).

c. Order of the German Eagle 1st Degree (Verdienstkreuz des Ordens vom deutschen Adler Erster Stufe).

d. Order of the German Eagle 2nd Degree (Verdienstkreuz des Ordens vom deutschen Adler Zweiter Stufe).

e. Order of the German Eagle 3rd Degree (Verdienstkreuz des Ordens vom deutschen Adler Dritter Stufe).

f. German Medal of Merit (Deutsche Verdienstmedaille).

The Meritorious Order of the German Eagle was not normally intended for award to German nationals, but some exceptions were made. The first German national to receive it was Constantin von Neurath, formerly Foreign Minister and later Reich Protector of Bohemia and Moravia. A 'Special Degree' (Sonderstufe) was presented on 20 April 1939 in recognition of his service as Foreign Minister. The same order

Paragraph 4 of the 20 April 1939 implementing order awarded a 'Special Degree' (Sonder-Stufe) identical to the Grand Cross in Gold to the Reich Protector of Bohemia and Moravia, Constatin von Neurath.[3] Even though the special award was not called by the same name, von Neurath was the first German to be authorized the Order of the Eagle. While such awards to Germans took place after this date, their numbers were extremely limited.

---

[3]*Uniformen-Markt, 15 May 1939, page 159.*

that established the 'Special Degree' award also served to bring about a revision of the previously established Orders. A new grade was introduced, and for the first time the addition of Swords was authorized. Even though the 'Special Degree' was supposed to be the highest level award among the recognized Orders as of this date, Hitler had already introduced yet another special award a year and a half earlier: the "Grand Cross of the German Eagle Order in Gold with Diamonds" (Grosskreuz des Deutschen Adlerordens in Gold und Brillanten). This one-time award was personally presented by Hitler to Benito Mussolini on 25 September 1937.[4] The breast star and sash Order were constructed by master-jeweller Godet of Berlin, while the sash was constructed by Karl Loy of Munich.

Mussolini is shown wearing his 'Grand Cross of the German Eagle Order in Gold with Diamonds' during Hitler's State Visit to Italy in May, 1938.

---

[4] *In an effort to determine the fate of this unique award, the widow of the former dictator was interviewed. She stated that the villa where this and other decorations (including the Pilot/Observer badge with diamonds) were located was occupied by partisans for over a year. Consequently there is no trace of the award since this time.*

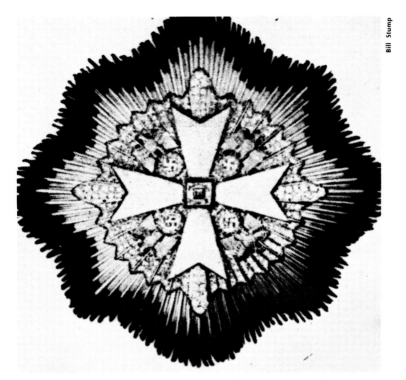

Breast Star of the Grand Cross of the German Eagle Order in Gold with Diamonds which was presented to Mussolini on 25 September 1937 by Hitler. This singularly unique award had a diamond studded starburst and a jewelled center. The actual cross inside the black border illustrated here is 3mm smaller than the 90mm original.

GRAND CROSS OF THE ORDER OF THE GERMAN EAGLE IN GOLD
(Goldenes Grosskreuz des Deutschen Adlerordens)

After Hitler had instituted the award on 20 April 1939, Italian Foreign Minister Count Galeazzo Ciano di Cortellazzo was the first recipient of the Grand Cross of the Order of the German Eagle in Gold (Goldenes Grosskreuz des Deutschen Adlerordens). Not only was Ciano the Italian Foreign Minister, but he was also the son-in-law of the Italian dictator, Mussolini. Ciano was a long-time supporter of the Nazis, and this honor was awarded to him largely for past diplomatic services. When the award was instituted, it was intended that only a maximum of sixteen be presented.[5] In fact, only eight were presented. Next in succession to receive the award was the Spanish Chief of State, Generalissimo Francisco Franco, followed by Admiral Horthy of Hungary (12 April 1942), King Boris III of Bulgaria (16 April 1942), President Risto Ryti of Finland (20 April 1942), Romanian Marshal Ion Antonescu, Japanese Ambassador

---

[5] *Uniformen-Markt* 15/1.8.40.

Count Ciano is presented the Grand Cross in Gold by Hitler on 22 May 1939. Here Hitler presents the red leather covered award document. The cased award is shown in the foreground.

Hiroshi Oshima, and the eighth and final recipient was Field Marshal Freiherr Carl Gustaf Mannerheim of Finland. The last award was rendered on 4 June 1942.

The Grand Cross in Gold consisted of an eight-pointed silver-gilt star measuring 91mm, and was worn on the left lower breast in conjunction with a 100mm shoulder sash with a 66mm sash cross.[6] Civilians were authorized the award without swords, while military personnel were awarded it with swords. In fact, it was on the 20th of April 1939 that all orders of the German Eagle Order were authorized to be awarded with and without swords. As mentioned previously, the addition of the swords connoted military service.

---

[6] *Dr. Heinrich Doehle (<u>Die Auszeichnungen des Grossdeutschen Reichs,</u> <u>1943</u>) states that the breast star measures 91mm.*

An order dated 27 December 1943 revised the grading of the German Order of the Eagle for the last time. Some of the major distinctions from the earlier awards were that the grades were designated 'class' rather than 'degree', and a white stripe was added to the center of the suspension ribbon of the bronze Medal of Merit. The finalized grades of the Order of the Eagle were as follows:

Golden Grand Cross of the German Eagle Order (Goldenes Grosskreuz des Deutschen Adlerordens) - with or without swords.

Grand Cross of the German Eagle Order (Grosskreuz des Deutschen Adlerordens) - with or without swords.

German Eagle Order 1st Class (Deutscher Adlerorden I. Klasse) - with or without swords.

German Eagle Order 2nd Class (Deutscher Adlerorden II. Klasse) - with or without swords.

German Eagle Order 3rd Class (Deutscher Adlerorden III. Klasse - with or without swords.

German Eagle Order 4th Class (Deutscher Adlerorden IV. Klasse) - with or without swords.

German Eagle Order 5th Class (Deutscher Adlerorden V. Klasse) - with or without swords.

German Medal of Merit (Deutsche Verdienstmedaille) - with or without swords.

(Refer to the following chart for description, designation, and comparison between the 1937, 1939 and 1943 series. The manner of marking found on each piece will determine which grade is which, as the marking system changed in 1939 and again in 1943.)

It should be noted that the width of the cross sash (Scherbe) and the width and placement of the stripes dictates the class to which the sash belongs. This size distinction is carried out throughout the various classes of the breast stars, etc.

Considerable emphasis is placed on the markings found on the various Orders as this is the only way to determine exactly what class the Order represents once it is removed from its original presentation case. The 'rule' for marking was sometimes not observed - largely for reasons of economic expediency. A 1943 5th Class Cross, for example, could be modified by adding the suspension loop, thus elevating it to the rank of the 3rd or 2nd Class. Under these conditions the original "5" mark on the fan would still remain.

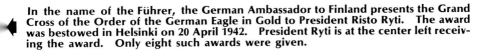

In the name of the Führer, the German Ambassador to Finland presents the Grand Cross of the Order of the German Eagle in Gold to President Risto Ryti. The award was bestowed in Helsinki on 20 April 1942. President Ryti is at the center left receiving the award. Only eight such awards were given.

One of the things that makes the Meritorious Order of the German Eagle so interesting (besides its relative rarity) are the various anomalies that exist. One rather subtle variation can be found on page 21 of Orders, Decorations, Medals and Badges of the Third Reich by David Littlejohn and Col. C. M.Dodkins. It should be noted that the four inner arms of the star are shorter. The standard pattern star for the Grand Cross had eight arms of equal length. Other variants for which there is not yet a suitable explanation are those produced with red enamel somewhere in the Order - either on the cross portion, the eagle portion, or both. It is possible that those Orders having the red enamel were intended for award to members of the SA, but never adopted. This, however, has not been substantiated.

A special award of the Grand Cross of the Order of the German Eagle in Gold was presented by Hitler to the German Foreign Minister, Joachim von Ribbentrop. The specimens shown here to exact scale were those actually awarded von Ribbentrop. (Photos courtesy Bill Stump)

Obverse of the 90mm breast star. All metal fittings are gold, while the cross and the areas surrounding the swastikas are white enamel.

The Spanish Foreign Minister and von Ribbentrop (Note his Grand Cross of the Order of the German Eagle in Gold).

Reverse of the breast star.   Unlike the smaller breast stars, the Grand Cross in Gold has the retaining hooks to support the massive weight.

1937	1939	1943
I. "Deutsche Ver-dienstmedaille". Title in Gothic script. Silver only. Without swords. Rim inscribed '835 PR. MÜNZE BERLIN'. Titling on reverse in upper and lower case. No ring marking. Red field on ribbon is solid. Medal measures 38mm. Ribbon is 39mm.	Addition of Swords authorized. The swords were mounted on the medal loop, and not on the face of the medal itself. Silver only. Other rim marks include 'Münzamt Wien 835'. No ring marking. Ribbon same as 1937 pattern. Swords are finished front and back.	"Deutsche Verdienstmedaille" title in Latin script. Title on reverse in upper case only. Bronze or silver. 38.5mm with or without swords. No rim marking. Ring marked '30'. Red field of 36mm ribbon has white stripe down center for bronze medal only. Because the base metal is sometimes zinc, both the silver and bronze may turn an overall gray color.
2. "Verdienstkreuz des Or-dens vom Deutschen Adler Dritter Stufe". Upper arm of the cross does not have the fan design, but simply a loop. Ring marked '900'. Red field on ribbon is solid. Ribbon measures 40mm, while the cross is 45mm. Worn suspen-ded from the left breast pocket.	Addition of Swords authorized. The swords were mounted on the enamel at the center of the cross. The cross design was modified to incor-porate the fan on the upper arm of the cross.	"Deutscher Adlerorden V. Klasse". With or without swords. Upper arm of the cross has a fan design. Fan is marked '5' to designate the class. Suspension ring is marked '21' to designate the manufacturer. Red field on ribbon is solid. Cross is 45mm.

dens vom Deutschen Adler Zweiter Stufe". Pin-back breast badge worn on left breast. Pin marked '900'. Badge measures 50mm wide.	authorized. The swords were mounted on the enamel at the center of the cross by means of a single rivet.	Deutscher Adlerorden IV. Klasse". With and without swords. Pin is marked '900' '21'. Base of pin marked '4'.
4. "Verdienstkreuz des Ordens vom Deutschen Adler Erster Stufe". Case title is 'Verdienstkreuz 1. Stufe des Ordens vom Deutschen Adler'. Cross is 50mm worn suspended from a 45mm ribbon worn about the neck. Cross loop is marked '900' and the grade designation '1'.	Addition of Swords authorized. The swords were mounted on the enamel at the center of the cross.	"Deutscher Adlerorden III. Klasse". With and without swords. Cross loop marked '900' '21', and fan is marked '3'.
5.	(Note: all breast stars were constructed with the cross affixed to the star by means of two rivets.)	When a recipient had already received a neck order, and was to be awarded the breast star for a higher award, just the breast star was presented. 'Stern des Deutschen Adlerordens'. With or without

6. "Verdienstkreuz des Ordens vom Deutschen Adler mit dem Stern". Six-pointed silver star measuring 75mm worn on the left breast. Neck cross measuring 50mm suspended from a 45mm neck ribbon. Pin of breast star is marked '900'. The case title is 'Verdienstkreuz mit Stern des Ordens vom Deutschen Adler'.	Addition of Swords authorized. The swords were mounted on the enamel at the center of the cross.	swords. Six-pointed silver star measuring 75mm. Worn in conjunction with the previously awarded neck order. Pin marked '900' '21'. "Deutscher Adlerorden II. Klasse. With and without swords. Pin to breast star marked '900' '21' while the cross loop is marked '900' '21' with a '2' on the fan pattern.
7. "Grosskreuz des Ordens vom Deutschenadler". Eight-pointed silver star measuring 80mm, worn on the left breast. A 60mm cross suspended from a 100mm shoulder sash. The red field on the sash	Addition of Swords authorized. The swords were mounted on the enamel at the center of the cross.	"Deutscher Adlerorden I. Klasse". With and without swords. Eight-pointed silver star worn on left (right*) breast. Pin marked '900' '21'. Sash cross measuring 50mm attached to a 90mm shoulder sash with a

center of the red field. Eagles are frosted silver rather than gilt. 'I' on upper arm ring.

8. "Grosskreuz des Deutschen Adlerordens". Eight-pointed silver breast star worn on the left side, measuring 80mm. A 100mm shoulder sash with a 60mm sash cross. With and without swords. Pin to breast star marked '900' '21'.

"Goldenes Grosskreuz des Deutschen Adlerordens". Same as 1939 pattern.

breast star.

9. "Goldenes Grosskreuz des Deutschen Adlerordens". Authorized on 20 April 1939, it consisted of an eight pointed gold (silver-gilt) breast star measuring 91mm, and a 100mm shoulder sash with a 66mm sash cross. Could be awarded with or without swords.

10. "Grosskreuz des Deutschen Adlerordens in Gold und Brillanten". A

special (Sonderklasse) award presented by Hitler to Mussolini on 25 September 1937. The breast star measured 90mm, and had eight points in gold. A second 'layer' consisted of a four pointed star studded in diamonds. The Eagle Order Cross was superimposed with a large center jewel. The 100mm shoulder sash was unique in the placement of the black and white stripes on the red field, and had a 66mm gold cross. Since this was a one-time award, it was presented only without swords.

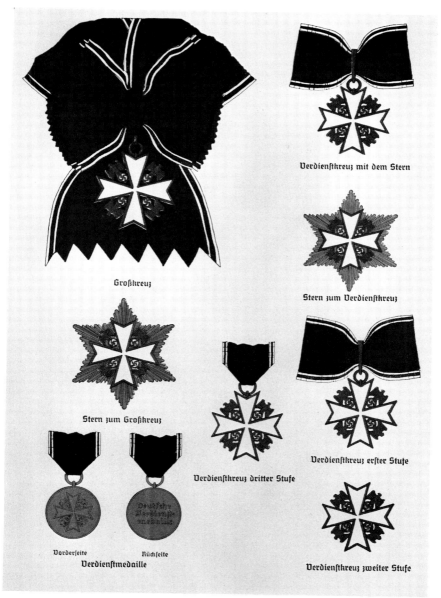

Großkreuz

Verdienstkreuz mit dem Stern

Stern zum Verdienstkreuz

Stern zum Großkreuz

Verdienstkreuz dritter Stufe

Verdienstkreuz erster Stufe

Vorderseite   Rückseite
Verdienstmedaille

Verdienstkreuz zweiter Stufe

AUTHOR'S NOTE: The 1937 edition of <u>Das Dritte Reich</u> illustrates the entire series of the 1937 Order of the German Eagle.   It should be noted that all crosses that were worn suspended were first produced without the 'fan' at the top arm.   It is suspected that the smaller suspension loop was found to be too fragile, and was reinforced by adding the 'fan' and making a thicker suspension ball.   In any event, the first pattern design of the 1937 series was short-lived.   Inspection of the first pattern neck cross indicates that the manufacturer's designation of silver content (900) was placed on the outer edge of the bottom arm.

46   **Sash and sash cross to the Grand Cross in Gold (not to scale).**

Sash Cross to the Grand Cross in Gold.   The sash was worn over the right shoulder, hanging diagonally across to the left side of the hip.   The sash cross was worn freely suspended just below the sash bow. Unlike the breast star, the sash cross was double-faced.   When worn properly affixed to the sash, the eagles would face to the left as shown here. The major difference between the sash for the Grand Cross in Gold and the standard Grand Cross sash is that the black band on the former measures 7mm, while the latter measures only 5mm.   Correspondingly, the outer white band on the Grand Cross in Gold is narrower.

Grand Cross of the Order of the German Eagle.   The star portion is silver, while the national emblems and the border of the cross are gold.

Reverse of the Grand Cross of the Order of the German Eagle showing manufacturer's proof code '21' and silver content number '900'.   Below the pin bar are two rivets that join the cross and eagles to the star.

Miniature of the Grand Cross of the Order of the German Eagle (twice actual size). This miniature was worn on the lapel chain when awards were authorized with civilian clothes and the wearer elected not to wear the full size award. The quality of the miniature compares favorably with that of the full size award.

Sash badge for the Grand Cross of the Order of the German Eagle. The reverse is identical to the obverse. All metal portions are gold.

1943 Eagle Order 1st Class. This award consists of an eight-pointed breast star and a shoulder sash with sash badge. The lower section of the interior is in two levels. The base level is for storage of the sash, while the upper level is a 'jeweler's' tray that is recessed for the breast star and sash 'badge.'

This Italian General wears the 193. Grand Cross of the Order of the Ger man Eagle during Hitler's State Visit to Italy in May, 1938.

1939 Order of the German Eagle with Star and Swords

Obverse of the 1943 breast star for the German Eagle Order 2nd Class with Swords. This breast star is identical to the award designated "Star of the German Eagle Order".

Reverse of the 1943 breast star for the German Eagle Order 2nd Class. Note that the pin is marked '900' '21'. This is only found on the 1943 awards, since the 1937/1939 awards are marked simply '900'.

1943 breast star in the original presentation case. The interior of the lid is white satin, bearing the designation 'Stern des Deutschen Adlerordens mit Schwertern' (Star of the German Eagle Order with Swords).

The 1937 Eagle Order 1st Class, the neck cross accompanying the 1937 breast star, the neck awards for 1939, the 1943 3rd and 2nd Classes are identical in design. Only the markings on the suspension loop and fan can determine the year and class.

53

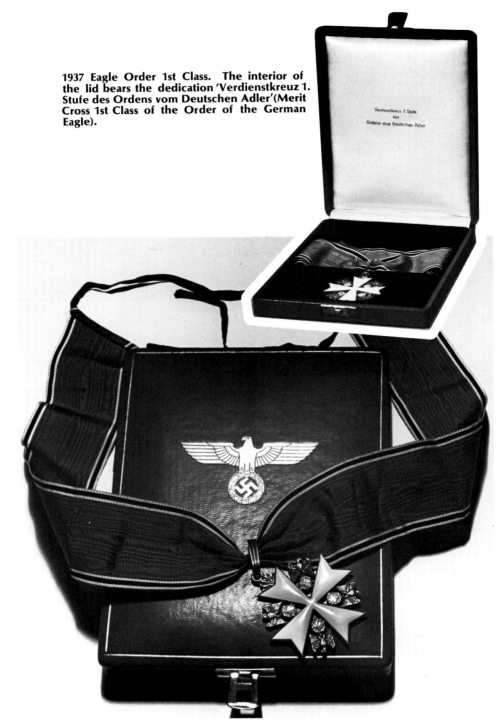

1937 Eagle Order 1st Class. The interior of the lid bears the dedication 'Verdienstkreuz 1. Stufe des Ordens vom Deutschen Adler'(Merit Cross 1st Class of the Order of the German Eagle).

Order of the German Eagle 1st Class (1937) with original presentation case. The outer case covering is red leatherette with gilt clasp, border and national emblem. The inside base is black velvet while the upper lid interior is white satin bearing the gold title 'Verdienstkreuz des Ordens vom Deutschen Adler Erster Stufe'. (Not to scale).

Generalleutnant Esteben-Infantes, Commanding General of the Spanish 'Blue' Division wears the Order of the German Eagle 1st Class.

O. Spronk

1937/39 2nd Class and 1943 4th Class designs were identical.

1939 Merit Cross of the Order of the German Eagle 3rd Class without swords.   The reverse design of the national emblems is identical to the obverse.   The reverse of the cross is white enamel.   The suspension ribbon is red with black and white outer stripes, measuring 40mm. The 1943 5th Class award without swords is identical in design.

1937 Eagle Order 3rd Class without Swords

The 1937 and 1939 pattern presentation cases for the 3rd Class were identical - red leatherette with a gold national emblem on the lid. The basic difference between these and the 1943 pattern case is the design of the eagle on the lid - the 1943 design being more elongated from wreath to head. The earlier award was designated 'Verdienstkreuz des Ordens vom Deutschen Adler Dritter Stufe' while the 1943 retained the same cross design, but was designated 'Deutscher Adlerorden V. Klasse'.

1943 German Eagle Order 5th Class with Swords. The design of the 1939 3rd Class with swords was identical. The reverse bears the same design less the swords.

Obverse of the 1943 Medal of Merit without swords. In most cases only the suspension ring is marked with the mint mark.

Bill Stump

Note the different pattern letters of the 1943 Medal of Merit with swords at the left compared with the 1939 award at the right. Note also that the reverse of the swords is finished identical to the front, and that the swords are fixed to the suspension loop rather than to the face of the medal. (This photo is not to exact scale.)

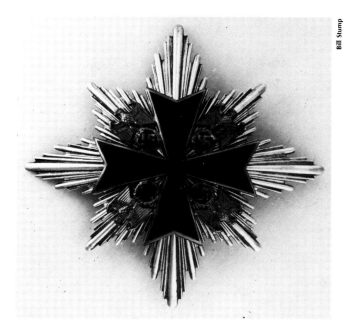

Two anomalies for which there is not yet an explanation.

1937-1939 Eagle Order award documents for awards without swords.

Points to be noted:

a. The title of the Grand Cross document is finished in gold leaf. All other printing is done in black. It was only necessary for the document to be signed by Hitler personally.

b. All subsequent award documents are done in black.

c. Note that the Eagle Order with Star is an awarded document.

d. All award documents (less the Medal of Merit) have the embossed national emblem in an oakleaf wreath, which is not distinguishable in these photos. The Medal of Merit has a distinctly unique seal embossed in the lower left hand corner.

e. The Medal of Merit was signed only by Meissner in the name of the Führer.

IM NAMEN DES DEUTSCHEN REICHES
VERLEIHE ICH

DAS GROSSKREUZ
DES ORDENS VOM DEUTSCHEN ADLER
BERLIN·DEN
DER DEUTSCHE REICHSKANZLER

Award Document for the Grand Cross of the Eagle Order.

IM NAMEN DES DEUTSCHEN REICHES

VERLEIHE ICH

HERRN DIVISIONSGENERAL

EZIO ROSI

DAS VERDIENSTKREUZ
DES ORDENS VOM DEUTSCHEN ADLER MIT DEM STERN

BERLIN·DEN 7. SEPTEMBER 1937
DER DEUTSCHE REICHSKANZLER

IM NAMEN DES DEUTSCHEN REICHES

VERLEIHE ICH

Award Document for the 1937 Eagle Order with Star, awarded to Italian General Ezio Rosi.

DAS VERDIENSTKREUZ
DES ORDENS VOM DEUTSCHEN ADLER ZWEITER·STUFE

BERLIN·DEN
DER DEUTSCHE REICHSKANZLER

DER CHEF DER ORDENSKANZLEI

Award Document for the Eagle Order 2nd Class.

61

STAATSMINISTER

IM NAMEN DES DEUTSCHEN REICHES

VERLEIHE ICH

DAS VERDIENSTKREUZ DES ORDENS VOM DEUTSCHEN ADLER ERSTER STUFE MIT SCHWERTERN

BERLIN·DEN

DER DEUTSCHE REICHSKANZLER

DER CHEF DER ORDENSKANZLEI

STAATSMINISTER

IM NAMEN DES
DEUTSCHEN
REICHES

VERLEIHE ICH

DIE DEUTSCHE VERDIENSTMEDAILLE
MIT SCHWERTERN

BERLIN/DEN

DER DEUTSCHE REICHSKANZLER

GEZ: ADOLF HITLER

DIE VERLEIHUNG
WIRD HIERMIT BEURKUNDET
DER CHEF DER ORDENSKANZLEI

STAATSMINISTER

Award Document for the Eagle Order Medal of Merit with Swords.

Award Document for the Eagle Order
1st Class with Swords.

LIFESAVING MEDAL
(Rettungsmedaille)

Reich President von Hindenburg reinstituted the Lifesaving Medal (Rettungsmedaille) as a national award on 22 June 1933. Originally a Prussian award, the medal dates back to 1833. A new design was created by the Federal mint in Berlin, which took the form of a 24mm round silver medal suspended from a yellow ribbon with white stripes. The obverse of the medal bore the German Federal eagle, while the reverse had the inscription 'Für Rettung aus Gefahr' (For Rescuing From Danger) surrounded by an oakleaf wreath. On 10 July 1937 a small swastika was added to the chest of the eagle, but otherwise the medal remained unchanged.

Obverse   **Reverse**

The award was open to all persons of good character over the age of eighteen who, not in the normal course of their daily duties (police, firemen, etc.), saved the life of a person in danger at the risk of their own lives. Military personnel were eligible for the award, but after the outbreak of the war, were more likely to be considered for a lesser military award such as the War Merit Cross. Non-Germans were also eligible to receive the award. Persons under the age of eighteen who qualified for the award were given a certificate of commendation, and were presented the medal upon reaching the age of eighteen.

At the time of institution, tentative regulations prescribed that it be worn on the medal or ribbon bar, ranked behind the service awards. In 1942, the subject of order of merit was raised, and numerous complaints were voiced stating that the medal was not given the degree of recognition commensurate with its degree of rarity. Regulations had still not been finalized by 1942, and it was acknowledged that the complaints would be taken into consideration, and noted that changes might be made upon finalization of the regulations. By 1943 the award was officially ranked behind service awards. The same regulations also prescribed that a ribbon could be worn in the

Obverse

(Not to scale)

Reverse

second buttonhole of the uniform jacket, providing the medal or ribbon bar was not worn.

As for the medal's relative rarity, only 165 awards had been rendered for all of 1936. The total number of awards is not known.

A non-portable award of identical design (but not suspended from a ribbon), measuring 50mm, was awarded under the same criteria for lifesaving of a lesser degree. A total of 248 of these awards was rendered in 1936.

An award document personally signed by Hitler accompanied the Lifesaving Medal, while the Minister of the Interior approved award of the Lifesaving Medallion.

Because two distinctive awards for lifesaving were created, a distinction of their titles was made:

a.   Lifesaving Medal (Rettungsmedaille am Bande)

b.   Lifesaving Medallion (Erinnerungsmedaille für Rettung aus Gefahr).

Award Document for the Lifesaving Medal.

Jn Namen
des
Deutschen Volkes
verleihe ich

für die Rettungstat vom
die Rettungsmedaille
am Bande.

Berlin, den

Der führer und Reichskanzler

The hard case that contains the Lifesaving Medallion has a gray exterior without any lid designation.   The upper portion of the lid has a white satin lining, and in the case of this particular example, the manufacturer's logo.   The lower portion is recessed to hold the medallion, and is finished in a burgundy velvet.

CROSS OF HONOR OF THE GERMAN MOTHER
(Ehrenkreuz der deutschen Mutter)

World War I exacted a heavy toll in war dead from the German male population. As a result, women were later pushed into factories to keep the wheels of German industry turning. Another result was that there were more marriageable women available than men, and thus a large number of women of child-bearing age remained 'unproductive'. Hitler took positive steps to solve the population 'problem'. One such program was to advocate the virtues of motherhood; this program included a gigantic propaganda campaign to urge women to increase the size of their families. Cash incentives were paid for each child born. The stigma of illegitimacy was removed since children born out of wedlock were to become wards of the State, and there were certainly willing girls more than happy to do their part for the Fatherland.

The propaganda campaign was given added stimulus on 16 December 1938 when Hitler instituted a new award to honor German motherhood, and especially the large family. The Cross of Honor of the German Mother (Ehrenkreuz der deutschen Mutter) was created in three classes with criteria as follows:

Hoover Institution

This German mother proudly wears her newly-presented Cross of Honor.

a. 3rd Class: A bronze Christian cross normally worn about the neck suspended by a 10mm blue ribbon with two white stripes at each edge. A round shield was affixed to the cross, bearing the inscription 'Der Deutschen Mutter' encircling a black enamel swastika on a white enamel field. Behind the shield and between the arms of the cross was a projection of rays. The arms of the cross were blue enamel with white enamel edges. The reverse was plain save for the date '16 Dezember 1938' followed by a facsimile of Hitler's signature. From 16 December 1938, when the decoration was first instituted, to mid-1939, Mother's Crosses bore the inscription 'Das Kind adelt die Mutter' (The child enobles the Mother). Why this change on the reverse of the cross was brought about is not known. The manufacturer's logo was sometimes found on the reverse as well. This award was presented, normally in a blue envelope bearing the designation 'Ehrenkreuz der deutschen Mutter Dritte Stufe', to mothers bearing four to five children. The award was accompanied by a large award document bearing a facsimile of Hitler's signature.

The 1st and 2nd design patterns were identical.

1st pattern (1938-39)

2nd pattern (1939-44)

b. 2nd Class: This was the same as above except that all metal parts were finished in silver; it was presented for bearing six to seven children.

c. 1st Class: This highly respected award was in gold, and was presented for bearing eight or more children.   Unlike the two lower classes, the award in gold was presented in a hard presentation case.

When the award was first instituted, approximately three million women qualified for one of these awards.   Only families of German origin qualified.   Females from Danzig, Austria and the Sudetenland were also eligible when these territories were absorbed into the Greater German Reich.   Awards were rendered only on 'Mothering Sunday' (or Mother's Day), the second Sunday in May.   The first awards were rendered on 21 May 1939, and the last awards were presented in 1944.

In addition to being worn about the neck, the cross was also worn in its full size suspended from a bow, and attached to the lapel.   A miniature, either suspended from a bow or made into a brooch, was also authorized.

All three classes were identical in size (35mm wide by 42mm high) and design, and were the creations of architect Franz Berberich.

The following series of photos shows the Mother's Cross in its production sequence, and is typical of any award having an enamel finish.

The cross is stamped from a sheet of bronze by a heavy die-press.

The inscription and facsimile of Hitler's signature is stamped on the reverse.   It is interesting to note that this author has an example in his collection that is void of inscription, which would indicate that it missed this step, and slipped through the inspectors to be awarded later.

The crosses are plated their respectiv[e] finish, and the enamel is added aft[er] the shield has been affixed to the cros[s]

After the enamel is added, the cross is placed on a screen for firing.

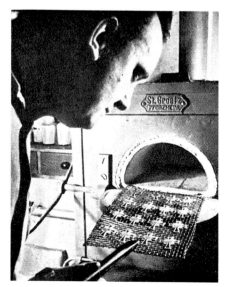

The enameled crosses are placed into a kiln under heat where the enamel is hardened.

The finished crosses are placed in their respective envelope or case, and the ribbon is added. This shows the finished silver 2nd Class Mother's Cross being packaged.

The presentation case for the gold 1st Class award was hard, hinged, and compartmented. The exterior was dark blue with a facsimile of the award in gold on the lid. The interior was white satin in the lid, and off-white velvet in the base.

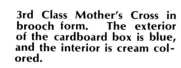

3rd Class Mother's Cross in brooch form. The exterior of the cardboard box is blue, and the interior is cream colored.

Standard pattern miniature worn on the left lapel or breast.   To exact scale.

A cased miniature, not to scale.

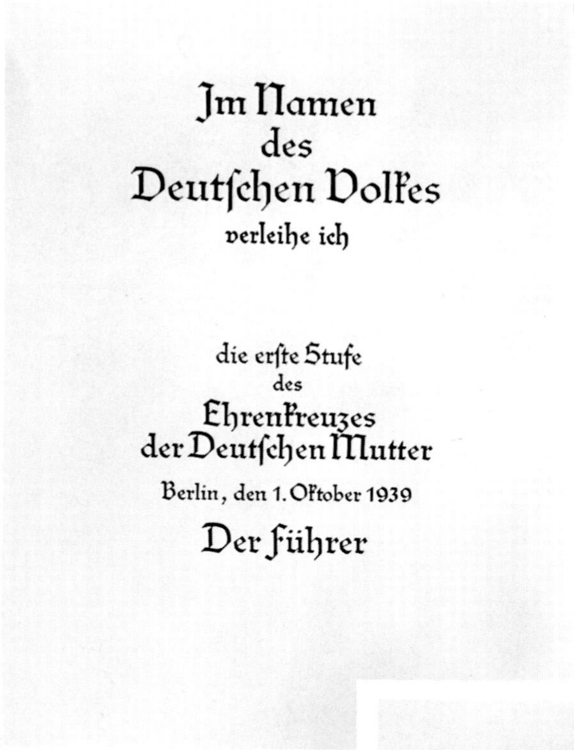

Jm Namen
des
Deutſchen Volkes
verleihe ich

die erſte Stufe
des
Ehrenkreuzes
der Deutſchen Mutter

Berlin, den 1. Oktober 1939

Der Führer

Award Document for the 1st Class Mother's Cross.

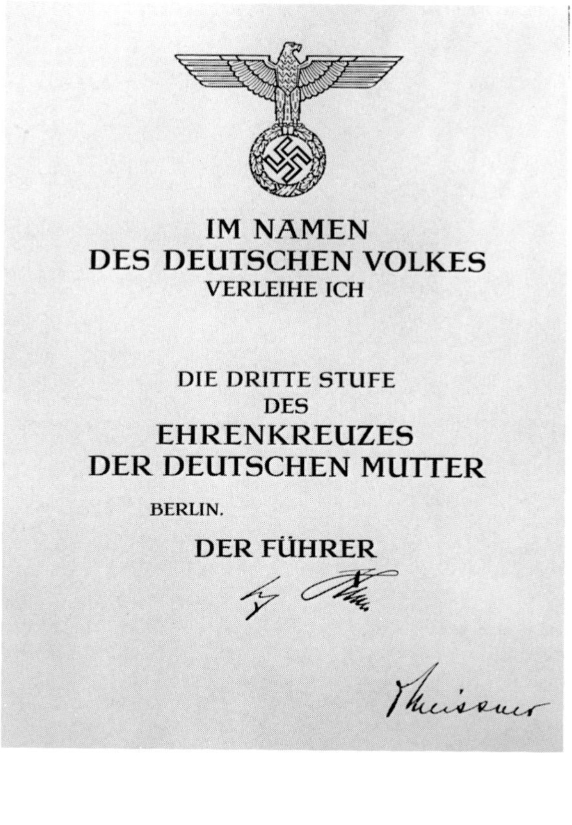

IM NAMEN
DES DEUTSCHEN VOLKES
VERLEIHE ICH

DIE DRITTE STUFE
DES
EHRENKREUZES
DER DEUTSCHEN MUTTER

BERLIN.

DER FÜHRER

Award Document for the 3rd Class Mother's Cross.

The requisites for this special Mother's Cross of Honor with Diamonds are unknown and it is included only as a point of interest. It is known, however, that the original recipient was a mother of sixteen children from Dresden.

Dragon's Teeth (Tank Obstacles) portion of the 'Siegfried Line'.

DEFENSE WALL HONOR AWARD
(Deutsches Schutzwall-Ehrenzeichen)

Hitler ordered that a medal be struck to recognize the planning and labor that went into the construction of the 'Siegfried Line' during the period between 15 June 1938 and 31 March 1939. The resultant medal was instituted on 2 August 1939, and was awarded to those members of the Armed Forces, including civilian employees in the hire of the military, who took part in the planning, construction, or defense of, German fortifications. A minimum time for construction workers was placed at ten weeks, while military assignment in a fortifications position only required three weeks.

The first medal was personally presented by Hitler to Armaments Minister Dr. Fritz Todt, on 23 November 1939. Following his award, other notable persons received the medal, including a few high ranking Luftwaffe and army generals as well as Konstantin Hierl and Dr. Robert Ley. Not including the first awards, a total of 622,064 was presented up until 31 January 1941. However, those members of the Armed Forces who had already received the Sudetenland or Memel Medals were not authorized to receive the Defense Wall Honor Award.

Dr. Fritz Todt, Armaments Minister and driving force behind the building of the West Wall, was personally presented the first award of the German Defense Wall Honor Award by Hitler on 23 November 1939. Congratulating him on the award is General Jacob, Inspector-General of the western fortifications. Other notable recipients on the same day were Hierl and Ley.

The medal was in one class only, and was suspended from a yellow/brown ribbon with white stripes. The obverse of the bronze medal showed a 'pill-box' fortification with crossed sword and shovel overhead surmounted by an eagle with outstretched wings. The outer edge of the oval medal was an oakleaf wreath. The reverse of the medal repeated the oakleaf wreath at the outer edge. Inside the wreath was the legend "Für Arbeit zum Schutze Deutschlands" (For Work on the Defenses of Germany). It was worn over the left breast pocket flap either as a ribbon bar or affixed to a medal bar.

Obverse   **Reverse**

Early strikes of this medal were made from solid bronze. However, those produced following the 1944 reinstitution order were made from zinc and colored with a bronze finish. The example shown is of the first production bronze series.

As the threat of an Allied invasion grew, Hitler ordered that Channel defenses be completed and improved. Immediately following the invasion, some 200,000 laborers were put to work improving and strengthening the 'Siegfried Line'. As a result, in an effort to spur on the labor force to complete their assigned task, Hitler reinstituted the Defense Wall Honor Award on 10 October 1944.

The following translation of an SS order provides an excellent definition of the requirements and procedures for award:

DEFENSE WALL HONOR AWARD

"Because of the Führer's proclamation on the reestablishment of the presentation of the German Defense Wall Honor Award, the following has been announced for the Wehrmacht and Waffen-SS inclusive:

The German Defense Wall Honor Award can be presented to members of the Wehrmacht and others not belonging to, but in the service of the Wehrmacht, who have been working for the establishment of the fixed defensive positions since the 6th of June 1944 which were to prevent danger from coming to the German people.

People who have sworn allegiance to the Führer as members of free foreign volunteers in the Wehrmacht also are authorized. Those who have received the German Defense Wall Honor Award at an earlier date will receive for the time since 6 June 1944, a bar to recognize additional duties.

In accordance with this regulation, members of the Waffen-SS scheduled to receive the German Defense Wall Honor Award from their respective groups must be submitted in a list (without reason for the award) providing family name, first name, rank, service, birthday and place of birth submitted in one copy to the SS-Führungshauptamt Adjutant".[7]

It is not known exactly what this bar was intended to look like, nor is it positive that it was ever put into production, much less actually awarded.

The medal is considered common since there was a total of over 800,000 awards made in two issues.

An award case for the German Defense Wall Honor Award was probably restricted to very special awards, and then only to the first series production. The case is a two-piece hinged construction fastened by a spring-tension release. The outer finish is a dark purple without anything on the lid. Inside the lid is purple/brown satin, while the lower portion is purple/red velvet.

---

[7]*Verordnungsblatt der Waffen-SS*, Berlin, 1 February 1945, Para. 60.

The most common form of presentation was a protective envelope. The envelope is tan with black lettering.

Deutsches Schutzwall-Ehrenzeichen

Im Namen des Führers und Obersten Befehlshabers der Wehrmacht

verleihe ich dem

Leutnant D r e w s , Alfred

das Deutsche Schutzwall-Ehrenzeichen

Wiesbaden, den   7. M a i   1940

Nr. 7487

Der Kommandierende General
und Befehlshaber im Luftgau XII

Dr. Weismann
Generalmajor

Award Document for the Defense Wall Honor Award, issued to a Luftwaffe Officer.

Professor Adolf Lorenz, the founder of German Orthopedics, receives the Goethe Medaille on his 90th birthday (22 April 1944). To his left is the Bürgermeister of Vienna, Ing. Blaschke.

National Awards (Non-Portable)

EAGLE SHIELD OF GERMANY
(Adlerschild des Deutschen Reiches)

Even though the Eagle Shield of Germany (Adlerschild des Deutschen Reiches) was a continuation (albeit with modified design) of an award instituted by Reich President Friedrich Ebert in 1922, the only reference found on it to date is contained in <u>Die Auszeichnungen des Grossdeutschen Reichs</u>, written by Dr. Doehle in 1943. Dr. Doehle does not mention this national award in his earlier publications, nor does he cite the date when the award designed in the Hitler era was instituted.

The award was to be presented to Germans, according to Dr. Doehle, "whose intellectual creations have benefited the German people". Approval rested with the Führer personally, and by 1 January 1943, only sixty awards had been presented.

O. Spronk

Dr. Erwin Guido Kolbenheyer stands in front of the Eagle Shield of Germany that was awarded to him for his participation in the fields of art, science, and literature. Author of numerous books, Dr. Kolbenheyer was recognized for his works in philosophy, art, and history.

The award in its original form was first presented to Gerhart Hauptmann on 15 November 1922, and was titled 'President's Eagle Shield' (Adlerschild des Reichspräsidenten). The first reference to the new Nazi Eagle Shield came when it was awarded to Richard Strauss on 11 June 1934 on the occasion of the noted composer's 70th birthday.

The shield, designed by H. Noack of Berlin, was a detachable round 110mm bronze medallion mounted on a bronze pedestal. The obverse of the medallion bore a large national emblem, while the reverse bore the recipient's name and citation.

Eagle Shield of Germany

GOETHE MEDAL FOR ART AND SCIENCE
(Goethe Medaille für Kunst und Wissenschaft)

The Goethe Medal for Art and Science (Goethe Medaille für Kunst und Wissenschaft) was founded in 1932 to reward outstanding service during the Goethe Centennial. It was initially intended to be a one-time award, but President Hindenburg retained it as a national award, and this practice was continued by Hitler.

The medal (not a medal in the true sense of the word, but a medallion) was silver, measuring 70mm, with the profile of Goethe on the obverse, and the name 'Goethe' to the right. On the obverse was a stylized national emblem over the inscription "Für Kunst und Wissenschaft" (For Art and Science). Engraved around the outer edge was the inscription "Founded by Reich President von Hindenburg 1932" (Gestiftet vom Reichspräsidenten von Hindenburg 1932). The Berlin sculptor Hanisch-Concee was responsible for the design of the medal. His 'signature' is found immediately under the neck of Goethe.

The earlier-produced medals had the recipient's full name engraved in large block letters around the edge. The proof mark '835 PR. ST. M. B.' (835[1] Prussian State Mint) was also present. The later pieces had the recipient's name in small block letters preceded by the date of award.

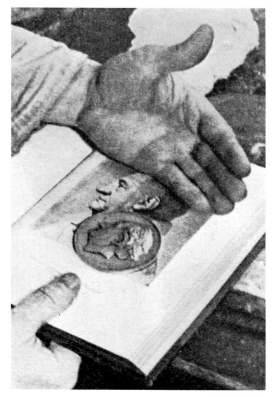

The Goethe Medal's design was based on this published portrait of Goethe.

---

[1]835 - *silver content*

Obverse

Reverse

The Goethe Medal continued to be awarded even after the introduction of the German National Prize for Art and Science in 1937, but took a subordinate position in relative merit. As of 1 January 1943 a total of 467 had been awarded. When presented, the medal was contained in a blue simulated leather hinged case with blue velvet base interior.

Note the recipient's name engraved on the rim of the medal.

IM NAMEN
DES DEUTSCHEN VOLKES
VERLEIHE ICH

DIE VON DEM VEREWIGTEN
HERRN REICHSPRÄSIDENTEN VON HINDENBURG
GESTIFTETE

GOETHE-MEDAILLE
FÜR KUNST UND WISSENSCHAFT

DER FÜHRER

Award document for the Goethe Medal for Art and Science (Unawarded).

Im Namen
des
Deutschen Volkes
verleihe ich

die von dem verewigten
Herrn Reichspräsidenten von Hindenburg
gestiftete
Goethe=Medaille
für Kunst und Wissenschaft
den
Der Führer und Reichskanzler

Variation of the Goethe Medal Award Document.

One of the National Winners in the 1944 National Trade Competition.

National Industrial Awards

VICTOR'S BADGE IN THE NATIONAL TRADE COMPETITION
(Siegerabzeichen im Reichsberufswettkampf)

The first National Trade Competition of the German Youth (Reichsberufwettkampf der deutschen Jugend) was instituted by Dr. Robert Ley, head of the German Labor Front, in 1934. Competitions were held annually every spring to determine the national winners in each field of competition. From 1934 to 1938, eligibility for the competitions was very restricted, and was limited to the following:

a. male laborers 15-18 years of age.

b. male commercial and technical apprentices 15-21 years of age.

c. females between 15 and 21 years of age.

d. students attending trade schools or commercial colleges regardless of age or sex.

(Additionally, all entrants had to be members of some Nazi-affiliated organization.)

Only one badge was awarded for each competition, and the winner was declared the National Victor (Reichssieger).

It was not until 1 May 1938 that eligibility was broadened and awards were increased to recognize competition winners at Kreis (local), Gau (state) and Reich (national) levels. Eligibility was expanded to include a wide spectrum of educational, commercial and industrial fields; the age restriction was removed and the Party membership requirement was lifted.

Initial tests were divided into three components including:

a. skill in the tested trade

b. political theory

c. mathematics and composition.

However, in 1938, the test criteria were changed somewhat, but remained primarily skill-oriented.

The largest competition was held in Cologne (Köln) from 22 to 29 April 1939, and was presided over by Dr. Ley and Reichsjugendführer Baldur von Schirach. Between them, they awarded 508 National Victor's Awards (Reichs-Sieger-Abzeichen). A total of 6,600 Gau and 40,000 Kreis awards had been presented previously in the qualifying contests.

The opening of the National Trade Competition in 1938.

Competitions continued to be held even after the outbreak of the war, but they were now referred to as 'Kriegsberufswettkämpfe', or War Trade Competitions. The last awards were presented in 1944 by Reichsminister Herbert Backe and Reichsjugendführer Artur Axmann, awarding a total of 406 National Victor's Badges between them.

Considering that the original criteria for award were considerably modified, and that some of the recipients were over 50 years of age, this award should not be considered a youth award but rather a national-level trade competition badge, as its title implies.

It is interesting to note that 6Pfennig and 12Pfennig stamps were issued on 4 April 1939 to commemorate the competitions and the award.

Stamps commemorating the 1939 Trade Competition badge.

The badges for the three levels of competitions were basically identical, consisting of a national eagle with outstretched wings, clasping a cog-wheel in its talons. On the cog-wheel was the red and white enamel Hitler Youth insigne. This was affixed to a round badge of white enamel with an oakleaf wreath. The major differences between the badges were as follows:

a. National level - all metal parts were finished in gold. Arched over the head of the eagle was the inscription 'Reichssieger'.

b. State level - all metal parts were finished in burnished silver, and bore the inscription 'Gausieger'.

c. Local level - all metal parts were finished in bronze and bore the inscription 'Kreissieger'.

Shown here are the Reichssieger and Gausieger badges won by Frau Teufel in 1938. She was not required to enter the Kreis competition, thus receiving no badge for this level. An example of the Kreissieger badge for 1938 is shown for comparison.

The 1944 badge differed from the prewar badges in that the white field and the HJ diamond utilized paint, rather than enamel, and the metal parts were alloys.

Each badge bore the date of the competition below the eagle's wings.

The reverse of each badge bore the manufacturer's logo. Those normally found are 'G. Brehmer, Markneukirchen', 'A. G. Tham, Gablonz a. N.' and 'H. Aurich, Dresden'.

Only the Reichssieger badge came in a presentation case (Gau and Kreis awards were boxed), but all were presented with an award document. The badges were not serial numbered.

The Reichssieger badge was presented in a black simulation leather hard case. The outer lid did not have any designation, nor did the inner white satin lining. The lower section was finished in vivid blue velvet. The other level awards were presented in a blue cardboard box with white interior.

2.Reichsberufswettkampf

der deutschen Jugend 1935

Beteiligungs-Urkunde

Deutschland ist durch Arbeit und Leistung
groß geworden. Die deutsche Jugend bekann-
te sich erneut zu diesen Idealen im 2. Reichsberufswettkampf 1935, an dem 1 Million
Jungarbeiter und Jungarbeiterinnen teilgenommen haben.

Mit einer guten Leistung hat sich an die-
sem Reichsberufswettkampf

Bruno Scharsenberg

aus der Gruppe **Bau** beteiligt,
worüber diese Urkunde ausgefertigt wird.

Heil Hitler!

Der Reichsorganisationsleiter der NSDAP   Der Jugendführer des deutschen Reiches
und Leiter der Deutschen Arbeitsfront

Participants' Award Document rendered to each participant in the 1935 National
Trade Competition.

Willi Piterzik

erwarb diese

Ehren Urkunde

für gute Leistungen
in der Wettkampfgruppe Druck und Papier
im

Berufswettkampf
aller schaffenden Deutschen

Berlin, am Tag der nationalen Arbeit
1939

Der Reichsorganisationsleiter   Der Jugendführer des Deutschen Reichs

Honor Award Document for Good Achievement in the category of Printing and Writing in the Professional Competition, 1939.

National-level award winners were often singled out for additional honors as a result of their success in the competitions.

Lack of war-time records precludes the establishment of an exact number of awards, but there were a total of 150,000 awards at the three levels given between 1934 and 1939.

EHRENURKUNDE

Charlotte Teufel

für besonders gute Leistungen im ›3.Reichsberufswettkampf der Deutschen Studenten‹ in der Reichssiegergruppe

Universität
Tübingen

DER REICHS-
STUDENTENFÜHRER:

MÜNCHEN-AM TAGE DER NATIONALEN ARBEIT-1938

Honor Certificate awarded to Frau Charlotte Teufel for award of the Victor's Badge in the National Trade Competition 1938.

Frau Charlotte Teufel, extreme right, prepares to receive the Victor's Badge in the National Trade Competition on 23 May 1938. At the age of 27 as a student attending Tübingen University Frau Teufel submitted a paper on the subject of the power of the Pope during the 7th century. The paper won first the Gau honors, and later went on to win the Reich honors. At the ceremony held in the Stuttgart Stadium she received both awards simultaneously. As a further honor, she was invited to meet Hitler at the Reichskanzelei late the same month. Her first impression upon seeing the Chancellor was, "He had blue eyes!" Frau Teufel was not a member of the NSDAP or Hitler Youth.

DECORATION FOR DEFENSE ECONOMY LEADERS
(Abzeichen für Wehrwirtschaftsführer)

The council for Defense Economy was established in January, 1938. Its members were chosen from among the leading industrialists in Germany. They represented every industrial field, and were entrusted with responsibility for the efficient conduct of industrial production and mobilization in support of the war effort.

The golden badge for Defense Economy Leader (goldenes Abzeichen für 'Wehrwirtschaftführer' or 'W Wi Fü') was instituted in March 1939, to recognize the members of the Council and to single out industrial leaders above the middle-management level who contributed significantly to the furtherance of industrial management.

97

Obverse

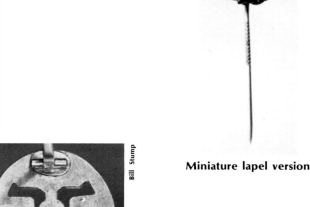

Miniature lapel version

Reverse

Recommendation for award had to come from the Kreis in which the proposed recipient worked, and had to be approved by the Oberkommando der Wehrmacht (OKW - military high command). It was worn on the left breast when the occasion called for civilians to wear orders and decorations (e.g., formal wear or designated wear.) A miniature version, differing slightly from the full-size badge, was worn on the left lapel.

The full-size badge was finished in gold (gold-colored aluminum or heavier base metal), measured 44-47mm high and 34-35mm wide, was oval-shaped, and had a vertical pin. The obverse of the badge depicted the national emblem surmounting a banner bearing the inscription 'Wehr-Wirtschafts-Führer'. Immediately below this was a factory complex belching smoke. The lower half of the oval was an open oakleaf wreath. (The reverse of the badge was either plain or sometimes bore a number.) The stickpin version bore the national emblem surmounting a banner with 'W Wi Fu' surrounded by an open oakleaf wreath.

How many awards were made is not known, but it is assumed that the number was very small. Among the recipients were Alfried Krupp, Kurt Tank, and industrialist Wilhelm Tengelmann.

PIONEER OF LABOR DECORATION
(Ehrenzeichen 'Pionier der Arbeit')

The last of the nationally recognized Party awards was the 'Pioneer of Labor'(Pionier der Arbeit), instituted by Hitler on 7 August 1940.   The first award was presented personally by Hitler to Gustav Krupp von Bohlen und Halbach, head of the Krupp munitions dynasty, on the occasion of his 70th birthday, 13 August 1940.   Subsequent awards were to be presented on Labor Day (1 May) and at the annual Nürnberg Party Rally.   Recorded awards were as follows:

1 May 1941

Max Amann, Reichsleiter and publisher

Dr. Wilhelm Ohnesorge, Reichspostminister (Minister of Posts and Communications)

23 September 1941

Dr. Robert Bosch, industrialist

1 May 1942

Prof. Dr. Ernst Heinkel, aircraft designer

Prof. Dr. Ferdinand Porsche, automotive designer of 'Volkswagen' fame

Walther Funk, Reichswirtschaftsminister und Reichsbankpräsident (Minister of Economics and National Bank President)

On 2 May 1942 Dr. Ley presents the Pioneer of Labor award to Prof. Heinkel.   Other recipients on this day were Prof. Porsche and Minister Funk.

Prof. Dr. Claudius Dornier, aircraft designer

Dr. Julius Dorpmüller, Reichsverkehrsminister (Reich Transport Minister)

Details of other awards are not yet known. However, it can be seen from this list of distinguished recipients that the total number of awards must have been very limited.

This high decoration was intended to be awarded to persons who were recognized for their exceptional achievement in industry and society. Competitions were held annually to determine the 'model plant' in industry. The owner or head of the winning plant received the 'Pioneer of Labor' award, and his plant was given the Golden Flag as a symbol of its achievement.

Basic pattern Pioneer of Labor decoration. Note how low the national emblem is set on the shield. This pattern has the horizontal pin.

 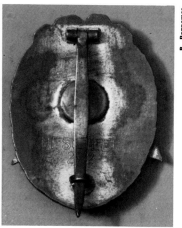

B. Regnemer

Variant pattern. Note how high the national emblem is set, and the vertical pin. The number below the manufacturer's logo may very well be the award serial number.

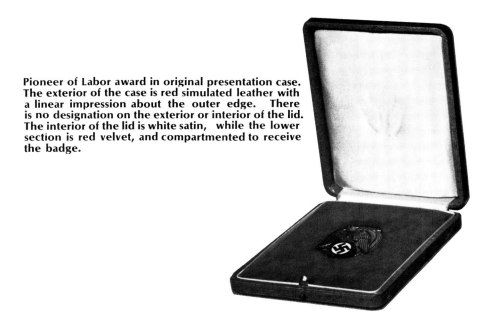

Pioneer of Labor award in original presentation case. The exterior of the case is red simulated leather with a linear impression about the outer edge. There is no designation on the exterior or interior of the lid. The interior of the lid is white satin, while the lower section is red velvet, and compartmented to receive the badge.

The 'Pioneer of Labor' decoration was designed by Professor Richard Klein. The oval badge measured 52mm high, and was 38mm at its widest point. Two minor variations were produced during the period, but both retained the same basic design, which depicted a stylized national emblem clutching the cog-wheel emblem of the German Labor Front. The DAF cog-wheel had a black enamel swastika on a white enamel field. The national emblem was affixed to a red enamel field surrounded by a gold laurel wreath, with a bow at the top. This basic pattern had the national emblem set low on the shield so that the cog-wheel projected below the wreath. A variant pattern had the national emblem set higher on the shield. The reverse of the basic pattern had a horizontal pin and a manufacturer's logo, whereas the variant pattern had a wide vertical pin and the manufacturer's logo.

The decoration was presented in a red leather case, and was accompanied by a very elaborate award document. The decoration was worn on the left breast pocket. No miniature is believed to exist for this decoration.

Approval for the award was vested in Dr. Ley, head of the German Labor Front.

DR. FRITZ TODT PRIZE
(Dr. Fritz-Todt-Preis)

In an order published on 12 November 1943, Hitler directed that a special achievement award be established to recognize persons in industry who had made a significant contribution to the war effort. The award was to honor Dr. Fritz Todt, driving

The Fritz Todt Award is presented for the first time by Reichsleiter Dr. Ley.

force behind the German autobahn system and the construction of the West Wall. The award was to be presented twice yearly, on 4 September, the date of Todt's birth, and 8 February, the date of his death. Dr. Todt's death in a plane crash on 8 February 1942 was viewed as a considerable loss to the German war effort.

The award came in three classes, and was only the second national award to carry with it a cash payment. The awards were as follows:

a. Gold: 50,000RM

b. Silver: 30,000RM

c. Steel: 10,000RM

The degree of the award presented was determined by the significance of the invention, improvement or general contribution to the war effort. Considering the cash award that accompanied by decoration, it is assumed that the Dr. Fritz Todt Prize ranked higher in merit than the Pioneer of Labor decoration.

The gold award was rendered only upon the joint approval of Dr. Robert Ley, head of the German Labor Front, and the Technological Department of the NSDAP. The first presentation was made by Dr. Ley on 8 February 1944.   This date is generally accepted as the date of institution of the award.

The badge measured 65-68mm high and 41-43mm at its widest point.   It took the form of an eagle sitting astride a banner bearing the name 'DR. FRITZ TODT' which surmounted the cogged-wheel swastika emblem of the German Labor Front.   A

Shown here is the 'Steel' Class (in reality, silver with a burnished finish for this example).   This high-quality specimen has open sections between the cogs that connect with the banner.   However, this is not normally found on the standard presentation pieces.   The reverse of this particular example bears the silver content number and the manufacturer's logo, whereas the standard piece is normally plain.

Obverse of the design variant.   This example is silver.
The reverse bears no markings whatsoever.

Reverse of the award in steel bearing the probable date of award and serial number. The clasp bears the manufacturer's code '21'. Slightly larger than exact scale.

Oddera

variation pattern of this badge was produced, and appears to have been awarded. The design of the variation was basically identical to the standard design except that the inscription on the banner read 'DR.-ING. FRITZ TODT-PREIS.' (See illustration). The reason for the two designs is not known.

The badge was awarded to the recipient in a presentation case, and was accompanied by an award document.

When worn, the badge was affixed to the lower left breast.

Col. Maitland-Titterton

BADGE OF MERIT IN THE AIRCRAFT INDUSTRY

A special lapel award for merit in the field of aircraft production was introduced in 1937. The Badge for loyal work in the industrial complexes of air travel (Treuewerkabzeichen der Betriebsgemeinschaften der Luftfahrt) was authorized for award to qualified civilian employees of the aircraft industry.

The award came in two classes - silver for merit and gold for outstanding achievement. Both awards retained the same design. Only found in stickpin form, since it was intended for wear by civilians on the civilian clothes, the award measured 25mm high and 15mm wide. A perched eagle with a 'T' crossed by a 'Wolfsangel' on the chest surmounted a white enamel shield with black swastika. The reverse of the award bore the designation 'Ges. Gesch.' or patent pending.

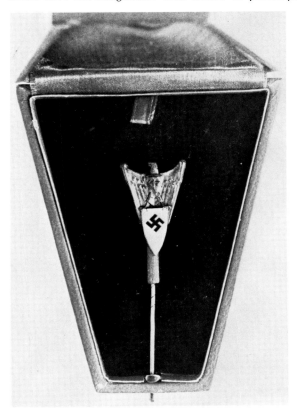

Presentation case
(not to scale)

This presentation case for the Dr. Fritz Todt Prize is green with the emblem of the DAF embossed in gold on the lid. Presentation was made with an ornate award document. A complete set of cased awards (Iron, Silver and Gold), which was obtained in late 1944 near Aachen by former staff sergeant Floyd Mock, has recently been acquired by this author. The cases all measure 105mm x 82mm x 25mm and are colored as follows: Iron is black colored, Silver is blue colored, and the Gold is red colored. Each interior lid is in white satin and marked 'Dr.-Fritz-Todt-Preis' in gold letters. The bases are black flocking and compartmented to hold the award.

Mussolini and Hitler in Munich, 1937. Note the Duce's Star of the German Red Cross.

Red Cross/ Social Welfare Awards

DECORATIONS OF THE GERMAN RED CROSS
(Ehrenzeichen des Deutschen Roten Kreuzes)

The Red Cross decorations were instituted by order of the President of the German Red Cross, and were national level, rather than state, awards. The history of the German Red Cross decorations dates back to April, 1922 - a time when the German Red Cross was the main organization tending to people's needs during periods of hardship. Prince Carl Eduard of Saxony-Coburg and Gotha became President of the German Red Cross (Deutsches Rotes Kreuz - DRK) following the death of Reichspräsident Generalfeldmarschall von Hindenburg, and, through his efforts, the status of the awards was elevated. In spite of this added recognition, the Red Cross awards were not authorized for wear on military uniforms until 1938.

The awards could be bestowed upon Germans and non-Germans who had made a significant contribution to the cause of the German Red Cross. Authority for approval of the award was vested in the President of the German Red Cross. (All this changed when Hitler personally intervened in the matter of the Red Cross awards in 1939.) In 1934 the Red Cross decorations had undergone a change in design in keeping with the emergence of National Socialist control over most aspects of German life. In 1937 ultimate control of the awards was placed in the hands of the Ministry of the Interior. This act of subordination resulted in yet another design change. In May, 1939, the Red Cross decorations were incorporated into the all-embracing series of Social Welfare decorations that had been instituted by Hitler. When this incorporation took place, Hitler decreed that all previous Red Cross decorations were superseded. However, this did not apply to the Sister's Cross of the Red Cross.

Thus, from 1922, when the decorations were first instituted, to 1939, when they were last authorized, the decorations of the German Red Cross had three different forms. These forms were as follows:

Form 1 (1922-1934):

a. 1st Class (erste Klasse): This was a neck award worn suspended from a red and white ribbon. The white enamel cross measured 51mm, and was bordered in gold. In the center of the cross was a round shield with a red enamel cross on a white enamel field. This was bordered by the inscription 'Deutsches Rotes Kreuz' (German Red Cross) in gold on a black enamel field. In cases of special awards a silver breast star was added to the 1st Class. When the star was presented, the 1st Class was worn about the neck, and the star was worn on the lower left breast.

b. 2nd Class (zweite Klasse): This award had the same basic design as the 1st Class, but measured 39mm. The 2nd Class Cross was worn suspended from a red and white ribbon on the left breast.

Form 1 (1922-1934) Red Cross Medal 2nd Class. All metal portions are gold. The front and back of the basic cross is white enamel, while the shield is red, black and white enamel.

Dr. Dorpmüller (center) wears the Star of the Grand Cross (1934) of the German Red Cross on his Government Official's uniform. Note also that Dr. Dorpmüller wears the Knight's Cross of the War Merit Cross about his neck during a gathering on 2 May 1944.

O. Spronk

Form 2 (1934-1937): Form 1 was changed on 30 January 1934. The Red Cross shield was replaced by the German national eagle without the swastika. On the chest of the eagle was a red enamel cross on a white enamel shield. All of the new awards were rendered with an award document. The newly-established Red Cross decorations were as follows:

a. Star (Stern): Awarded for exceptional achievement, the star was worn on the lower left breast. It was a standard pattern DRK Cross measuring 47mm affixed to a 72mm four-pointed silver star. Each ray of the star was bordered by a rope-like pattern. In recognition of still more exceptional service, authorized recipients could wear a shoulder sash in conjunction with the star. When so authorized, the sash was worn over the right shoulder and across the left hip.

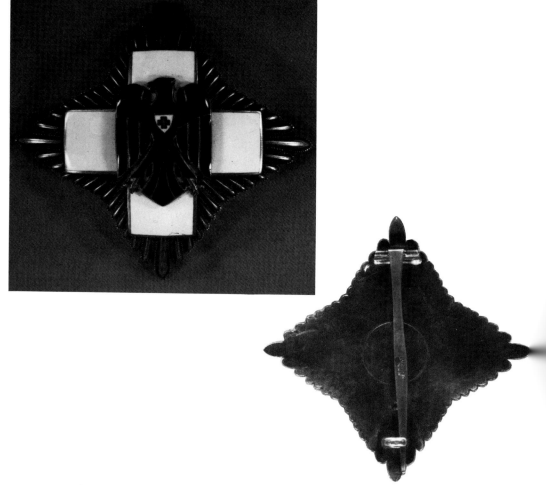

2nd Form (1934-1937) Star of the German Red Cross. The German Red Cross national eagle was in black enamel outlined in gold on a white enamel cross. The cross was riveted to a four-pointed silver star.

This Special Class Award in presentation case (left) was taken from Mussolini's villa at Lake Garda by Lt. Col. William S. Lueck, of the 19th Mountain Division on April 29, 1945. The exterior of the case is red without lid designation and the interior base is black velvet.

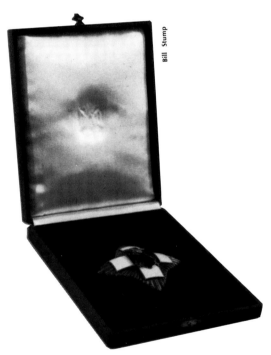

Bill Stump

The presentation case for the 2nd Form Star was simulated red leather with no lid designation. Interior of the lid was white satin, while the base was dark blue velvet.

Obverse of Mussolini's Sash Decoration.

Reverse of Mussolini's Sash Decoration (not to scale).

b. 1st Class (Erste Klasse):   This was a standard pattern DRK Cross, measuring 54mm and worn about the neck.   The Cross was suspended from a red and white ribbon by means of a ribbed suspension loop.

c. Cross of Merit (Verdienstkreuz):   This was a 51mm vaulted Cross worn on the left breast pocket.   The reverse was completely plain.

d. Decoration of the Red Cross (Ehrenzeichen des Roten Kreuzes):   A 39mm Cross worn suspended from a red and white ribbon on a medal bar above the left breast pocket.   The reverse was completely plain.

e. Ladies' Cross (Damenkreuz):   Same as (d.) above, except that the Cross was worn suspended from a red and white bow ribbon on the upper left breast.   The Decoration of the Red Cross and the Ladies' Cross were equal in rank.

Form 3 (1937-1939):   The design underwent still another change on 6 April 1939 when the 1934 pattern eagle was replaced by another eagle clutching a swastika within a wreath.   With the design change came two additional grades.   The seven grades were as follows:

a. Grand Cross (Grosskreuz):   A 54mm DRK Cross on a four-pointed silver star worn on the lower left breast.   The star was worn in conjunction with a 96mm red and white shoulder sash which had a 54mm DRK Cross suspended over the left hip.

b. Star: Same as (a.) above, but worn without the cross sash.   It was worn on the lower left breast.

Bill Stump

Star of the German Red Cross, Form 3 (1937-1939)
The 47mm DRK Cross was riveted to a 72mm four-pointed silver star, and worn on the lower left breast.   It should be noted that most of these breast stars have been encountered with both rounded (as illustrated) and pointed star tips.

Form 3 Star being worn by an SA-Obergruppenführer attending the national Labor Day rally in 1937.

    c.   1st Class: A 54mm DRK Cross worn about the neck, suspended from a red and white ribbon by a loop with three gold oakleaves.   The reverse of the 1st Class Cross was plain.

    Under special circumstances, a First Class decoration with diamonds was awarded to noted women who had made a significant contribution to the Red Cross.   The Grand Duchess Sophie Charlotte of Luxemburg, Princess Olga of Yugoslavia, Crown Princess Elena of Italy and the mother of King Farouk of Egypt were among the few recipients of this award.   To create this variant, diamonds (Brillanten) were added to the arms of the Cross, covering them completely or merely bordering the edges.   This decoration set the pattern for the First Class award with diamonds of the Social Welfare Cross which would follow in 1939.   Female awards were worn suspended from a red and white bow-ribbon on the left breast.

    d.   Cross of Merit: A vaulted 51mm DRK Cross worn on the lower left breast.   The reverse was plain.

    e.   2nd Class: A 39mm DRK Cross identical to the 1934 pattern Decoration of the Red Cross, but with the newly designed eagle.   This award was worn suspended from a 28-30mm red ribbon with white outer edges.   The reverse was completely plain.

    f.   Women's Cross (Frauenkreuz):   Identical to the 2nd Class decoration, except that it was worn suspended from a bow-ribbon on the upper left breast.

114

1937 Pattern 1st Class Red Cross decoration.

Members of the diplomatic corps stand in attendance during the signing of the New Year register by General Oshima, Japanese Ambassador to Germany. Two members of the German diplomatic corps wear the 1937 Pattern of the German Red Cross Cross of Merit (Verdienstkreuz).

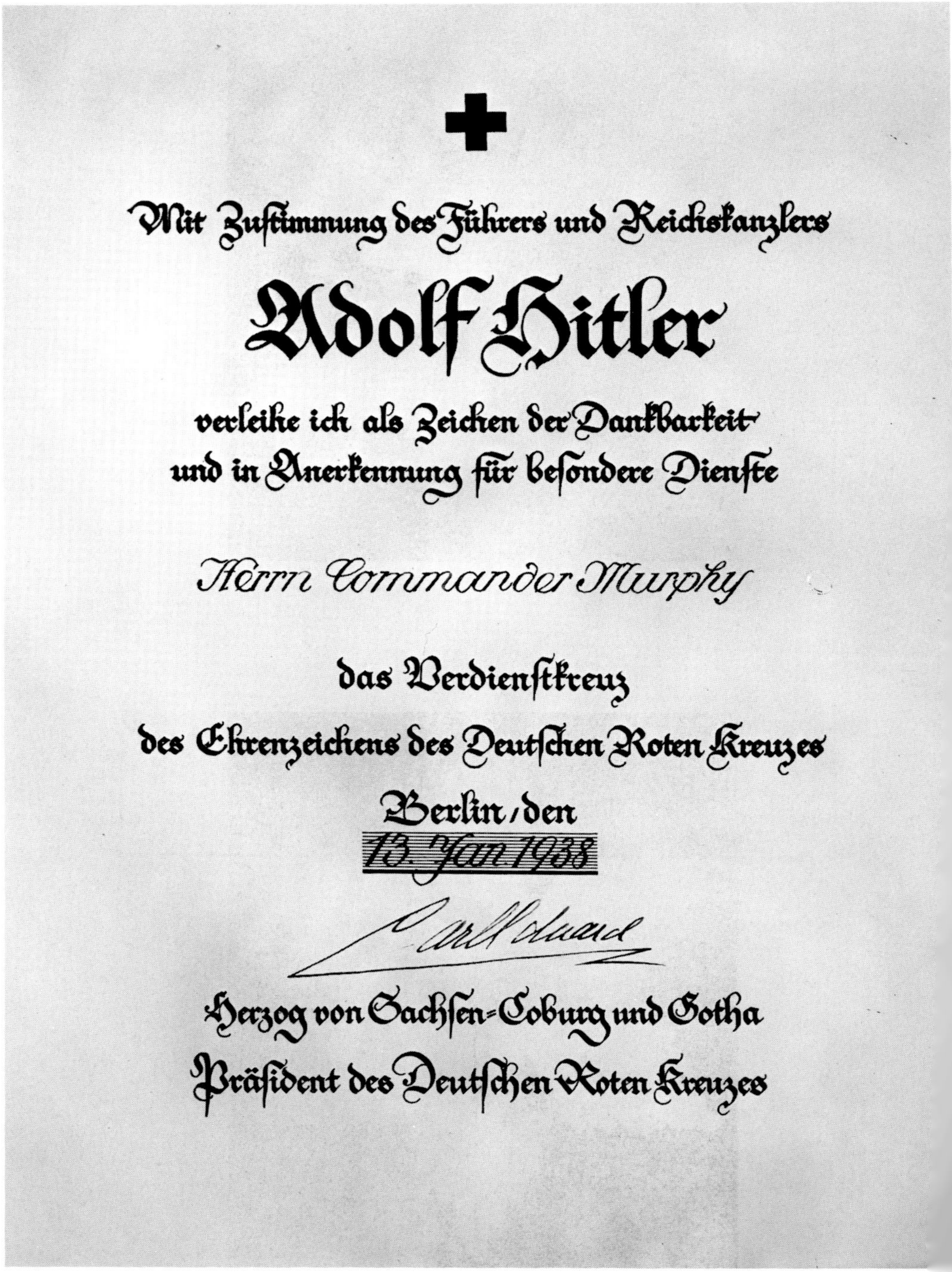

✝

Mit Zuſtimmung des Führers und Reichskanzlers

Adolf Hitler

verleihe ich als Zeichen der Dankbarkeit
und in Anerkennung für beſondere Dienſte

Herrn Commander Murphy

das Verdienſtkreuz
des Ehrenzeichens des Deutſchen Roten Kreuzes

Berlin, den
13. Jan 1938

Carl Eduard

Herzog von Sachſen-Coburg und Gotha
Präſident des Deutſchen Roten Kreuzes

Award Document for the 1937 Cross of Merit awarded to a British Naval Commander. The authorization letter on the next page is self-explanatory.

Any further communication
should be addressed to—
The Secretary of the Admiralty,
London, S.W.1.
quoting C.W.6546/38.

L.P.—No. 8

Admiralty, S.W.1.

9th June, *193* 8.

Sir,

      I am commanded by My Lords Commissioners of the
Admiralty to inform you that His Majesty the King has
been pleased to grant you permission to wear, without
restriction, the Order of the German Red Cross conferred
upon you by the German Government in recognition of your
services to the wounded members of the crew of the German
battleship DEUTSCHLAND at Gibraltar.

      I am, Sir,

          Your obedient servant,

          H Eastwood

Commander H.J. Murphy, R.N.,
    United Services Club,
      Pall Mall,
        London, S.W.1.
B.

1937 Pattern Women's Cross. The 2nd Class Cross was identical to this, but worn by men suspended from a straight 28-30mm red and white ribbon.

g. Medal of the German Red Cross (Medaille des Deutschen Roten Kreuzes): A 38mm round medal worn suspended from a red and white ribbon on the medal bar above the left breast pocket.   The medal had a red translucent enamel DRK Cross with the DRK eagle in the center.   This was surrounded by a silver outer circle.   The reverse carried over the basic design, but instead of the DRK eagle there was the inscription 'Für Verdienste um das Deutsche Rote Kreuz' (For Service in the German Red Cross).

It is interesting to note that the DRK regulations specifically state that the DRK awards were patented designs.

Those Red Cross awards classified as a decoration were required to be returned to the German Red Cross upon the death of the recipient.

Obverse   **Reverse**

1937 Medal for the German Red Cross

GERMAN RED CROSS SISTER'S CROSS
(Deutsches Rotes Kreuz Schwesternkreuz)

Since neither the awards of the German Red Cross (Deutsches Rotes Kreuz - DRK) or the later German Social Welfare (Deutsche Volkspflege) were specifically intended for recognition of loyal service, four long service awards (Dienstleistungsabzeichen) were created on 1 July 1937 to recognize the service of Sisters and Matrons. The awards were as follows:

a. For 10 Years Service as a Sister: A 50mm silver cross suspended from a neck chain. At the center of the cross is a 22mm round DRK insigne in black, red and white enamel with silver highlights. The reverse is plain except for a possible manufacturer's proofmark.

b. For 25 Years Service as a Sister: Identical to the above, but with an oakleaf wreath encircling the DRK insigne.

c. For Long Service as a Matron: Same as (a) above except that the cross is gold.

d. For Long Service as a Senior Matron: Same as (b) above except that the cross is gold.

As these were service awards, they remained unaffected by the order of May 1939 which established the new awards of the German Social Welfare. Award of the DRK Sister's Cross (Schwesternkreuz) continued until the end of the war.

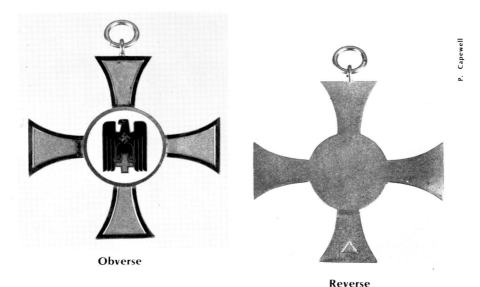

P. Capewell

Obverse

Reverse

The 10-year service award for the DRK Sister and the Long Service award for the Matron was in silver, while the 25-year service award for the DRK Sister and the Long Service award for the Senior Matron was in gold. The latter two awards had the addition of the oakleaf wreath about the center insigne. Note the manufacturer's logo on the lower reverse arm, and the variation suspension ring.

The reverse of a standard pattern DRK Sister's Cross showing the front insigne attachment rivet and the more common suspension loop.

25 Years Service as a Sister. The reverse is plain except for a manufacturer's logo in the form of a triangle.

There were other distinctive devices worn by members of the DRK which did not qualify as awards. These were as follows:

a. Active Membership brooch for the DRK Sister. This was an enamel pin in red, black and white with silver highlights which was worn at the throat. The reverse bears the manufacturer's logo, the DRK location and the serial number.

b. DRK Helper (Helferin): This was a brooch worn at the throat which came in three degrees:

c. Badge of Honor of the DRK (Ehrennadel des DRK): This 28mm round badge came in the form of a pin worn on the lapel. It was awarded for merit which did not warrant award of the Red Cross or Social Welfare decorations. The center motif was the national emblem of the DRK - a black eagle clutching a red cross with a silver swastika on its chest. The insigne was surrounded by an oakleaf wreath. The reverse is plain except for the manufacturer's logo. It was also produced in a stickpin version.

Active Membership brooch

Magda Darchinger, a Red Cross Sister, wearing a variation of the Membership Brooch at her throat.

Senior Helper

Helper

Beginning Helper

Badge of Honor
of the DRK

GERMAN SOCIAL WELFARE DECORATION
(Ehrenzeichen für Deutsche Volkspflege)

With a Hitler-order of 1 May 1939 all Red Cross awards were superseded by the newly introduced German Social Welfare decoration (Ehrenzeichen fur Deutsche Volkspflege). The new awards were introduced because Hitler felt that they should cover the whole field of social welfare, and not just the relatively restricted area of the Red Cross. Hitler specified that the award would come in four classes, and would be rendered in recognition of loyal service in connection with the following:

    a. Social Welfare

    b. Winter Relief

    c. Looking after the sick and wounded, both in peace and war

    d. Keeping up the old customs

    e. Looking after German nationals in foreign countries.

This series of awards was not to be extended to members of the Luftschutz or Fire Departments, since they had awards of their own to recognize this type of service.

Final approving authority was vested jointly in the President of the Red Cross, Reich Minister of the Interior, Reich Labor Minister, Reich Minister for Propaganda, and the Chief of the OKW (Military High Command).

Hauptamtsleiter SS-Gruppenführer Erich Hilgenfeldt became the first recipient of the 1st Class decoration on 17 August 1939 in recognition of his services to the Winter Relief. The first awards of the medal were not rendered until Christmas, 1939.

When the war broke out in September, 1939, greater emphasis was placed on the military. Regulations published in December of that year governed the award of these decorations to military personnel, and placed certain restrictions on their bestowal. Awards were to be presented to the military in the following manner:

a. 1st Class to general officers.
b. 2nd Class to Colonels (Oberst) and Lieutenant Colonels (Oberstleutnant).
c. 3rd Class to Majors and Captains (Major und Hauptmann).
d. Medal to Lieutenants (Leutnant) and below.

Specifications restricting awards to a certain rank within the military were not uncommon throughout the world, and remain a practice today. Regulations specified that the German Social Welfare decoration could not be awarded to a military person if his service would qualify him for an award of the War Merit Cross or other military award.

As the war progressed, Hitler authorized the addition of swords (normally characteristic of war-time awards) to the suspension ribbon. However, in reality these were added only to the 3rd Class and the medal, since the 2nd Class was a breast badge and the 1st Class was a neck order. The new addition did not result in a newly designed decoration, but was achieved simply by adding crossed silver swords to the suspension ribbon of the medal and crossed gold swords to the 3rd Class ribbon. An order instituting the swords was dated 30 January 1942.

In September of that year a 1st Class award inlaid with diamonds (Brillanten) was awarded to Madame Antonescu, wife of the Romanian dictator. This award was in brooch form, and was to be worn on the upper left shoulder. It is not known if further awards of this type were rendered, but it can be assumed that such awards were intended to be presented to women of high rank who had made a significant contribution to the cause of social welfare. This award is currently on permanent display at the US Military Academy at West Point, New York.

Exactly when the Special Grade Social Welfare decoration was introduced is not known, but it became the sixth award in the series, and ranked as the highest in recognition. After 1942, the series of the Social Welfare awards was as follows:

Special Class (Sonderstufe): An 84mm four-pointed breast star identical to the 1937-1939 pattern Grand Cross except that the 'Volkspflege' (Social Welfare) insignia was attached to the white enamel cross. This was worn on the lower left breast in conjunction with a 100mm wide cross-sash which suspended a decoration identical to the 1st Class award. The 1st Class neck award could be worn at the same time as the Special Grade award.

1st Class with Diamonds (1. Stufe mit Brillanten): Only one such award is known to have been presented, and that to Madame Antonescu. It was designed to be worn on the left shoulder as a brooch suspended from a bow. The area of the cross which was normally white enamel was studded with diamonds, as was the oakleaf suspension loop. The award was presented with a very ornate award document and binder. Both the award and the binder were the creations of Frau Gerdy Troost, whereas all other awards in the Social Welfare series were designed by Professor Richard Klein.

Special Class of the Social Welfare Decoration Breast Star. It should be noted that this and earlier breast stars were produced with rounded (illustrated) and pointed tips.

Reverse of the Special Class breast star. The presentation engraved here would indicate that this award was personally presented to Dr. Gerhard Wagner on 20-4(April)-(19)43, the date of Hitler's birthday. Dr. Wagner was a member of the Reichstag and Reichsführer of the German Doctor's League.

German Social Welfare Decoration 1st Class with Brilliants. (Specimen shown is that which was awarded to Madame Antonescu.)
Photos courtesy of the West Point Museum Collection.

(not to scale)

a. Obverse. Diamond arrangement is as follows - bottom arm 24, top arm 22, right arm 20, and left arm 20. Not included are small diamond chips spaced between the major stones. Diamonds are also included in the design of the Oakleaf suspension device.

125

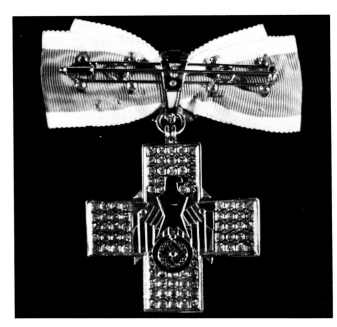

b. Reverse. Note the unique pin assembly.

c. Reverse of the Oakleaf suspension showing hinged device and manufacturer's logo (Klein) and content numbers.

e. Lid of special case. The basic case is silver (925) with a gold national emblem, and an outer design border of alternating gold design and what may be diamond gem stones.

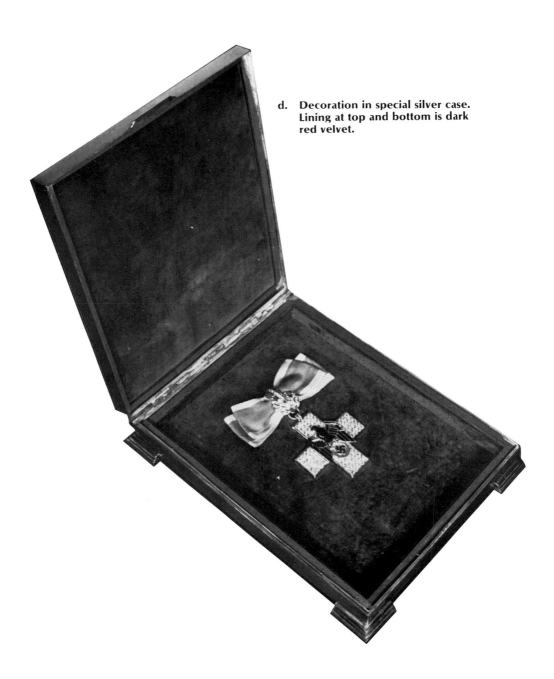

d. Decoration in special silver case. Lining at top and bottom is dark red velvet.

1st Class (l. Stufe):   A 52mm cross worn suspended from a gold ribbed suspension loop with two oak leaves.   The cross was suspended from a red and white 56mm ribbon worn about the neck.   Usually, the reverse of the cross is solid white enamel, but original examples may have existed bearing the manufacturer's logo on a plain gold-plated surface.

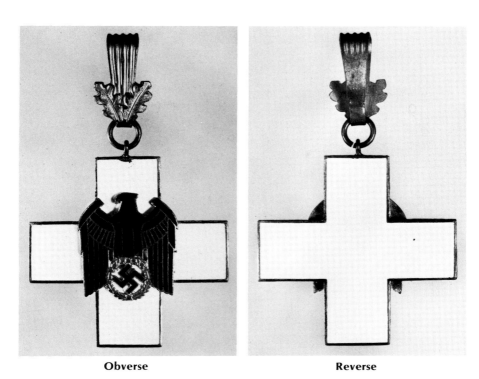

Obverse   Reverse

The example shown is a war period production example with the narrow
suspension loop at the top of the cross. Earlier examples had a thick
'ball' suspension connecting the suspension ring.

The presentation case for the 1st Class
award was red with blue satin lining in
the lid, bearing the title of the award in
gold. The lower section of blue velvet
was compartmented and recessed to
accept the cross. Some cases have a
provision for a small lapel ribbon just
below the cross.

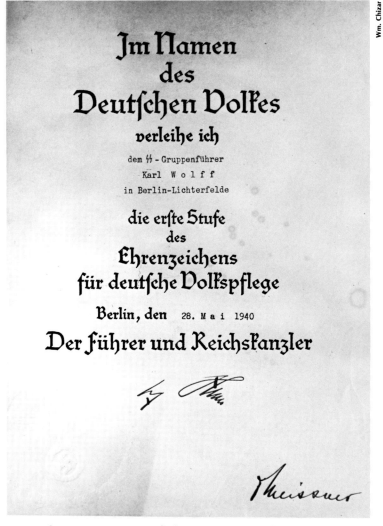

Jm Namen des Deutschen Volkes

verleihe ich

dem ᛋᛋ - Gruppenführer

Karl W o l f f

in Berlin-Lichterfelde

die erste Stufe des Ehrenzeichens für deutsche Volkspflege

Berlin, den 28. M a i 1940

Der führer und Reichskanzler

1st Class Document awarded to SS-Gruppenführer Karl Wolff.

2nd Class (2. Stufe): A 52mm cross in pin-back form worn on the left breast pocket. This class was produced in both the flat and vaulted forms, and occasionally bore the manufacturer's logo.

3rd Class (3. Stufe): A 40mm cross worn suspended from a 35mm red ribbon with white edges. Male recipients wore it on the medal bar over the left breast pocket, while female recipients wore it suspended from a bow in brooch form on the upper left shoulder. It could be worn with crossed gold swords on the ribbon.

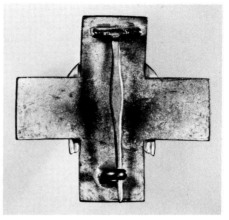

Obverse   Reverse

2nd Class Social Welfare Decoration

Reverse of the pin-back 2nd Class award with the name of the female recipient and the date of award.

Medal (Medaille):   A 38mm round dull-silver medal suspended from a 30mm wide red ribbon with white edges.   The obverse bore the insignia of the Social Welfare, while the reverse bore the inscription 'Medaille für deutsche Volkspflege' (Medal for German Social Welfare).   The award was worn in the same manner as the 3rd Class, and could be worn with crossed silver swords.

After the introduction of the Social Welfare decoration, the Red Cross decorations could still be worn, unless the person involved was subsequently awarded a Social Welfare award of equal rank, in which case this was worn.   131

3rd Class German Social Welfare Decoration as worn by female recipients.

German Social Welfare Decoration 3rd Class.   The presentation case has a red exterior with a gold line running about the edge of the lid, but bears no lid designation.   The interior of the lid is dark blue satin with a satin band bearing the designation 'Ehrenzeichen für deutsche Volkspflege 3. Stufe' (Decoration for German Social Welfare 3rd Class), and serves to retain the suspension ribbon.   The base is dark blue velvet, and is compartmented to receive the cross.

Obverse of the Medal as worn by female recipients.

Reverse of the Medal
as worn by men.

Award packet for the Medal for German Social Welfare. The packet is cream colored with black title. (Exact scale)

Im Namen des Deutschen Volkes

verleihe ich

Kreisamtsleiter Karl Franck,
Aalen,

die

Medaille
für deutsche Volkspflege

Berlin, den 30. Januar 1940

Der Führer und Reichskanzler

Award document for the medal for German Welfare

IM NAMEN
DES DEUTSCHEN VOLKES
VERLEIHE ICH

DIE
MEDAILLE
FÜR DEUTSCHE VOLKSPFLEGE
BERLIN,

DER FÜHRER

Second pattern award document for the Social Welfare Medal. The document shown (not to scale) is unawarded, and is part of the collection assembled by Dr. Doehle in support of his archives on his country's awards and decorations.

Only one class could be worn at any given time. When the recipient was awarded a higher award, the lower award had to be returned to the Department of Orders and Decorations; however, awards were retained by the family upon the death of the recipient.

Service Awards

Heinrich Himmler, wearing his SS Long Service Award, is shown meeting Spanish delegates in September, 1940.

HONOR BADGE OF THE TECHNICAL EMERGENCY SERVICE
(Ehrenzeichen der Technischen Nothilfe)

The Technical Emergency Corps (Technische Nothilfe - TN or TeNo) was formed on 30 September 1919 to serve as a voluntary organization to perform stand-by duty in the event of a general strike that might threaten Germany. Under Hitler it evolved into a large emergency force complete with a salaried cadre. In 1937 it was absorbed by the Police organization, and as a result, later by the SS network.

A special membership pin was created for the TeNo in the winter of 1934, but this proved inadequate to recognize the long service of some of its members. On 2 April 1935 the Honor Badge of the Technical Emergency Corps (Ehrenzeichen der Technischen Nothilfe) was instituted to single out long-standing members who had significantly contributed to the organization and its aims. The award was limited to members who had joined the TeNo between 1919 and 1923 inclusive. The first award was presented on 1 October 1935. The total number of awards is not known, but it is assumed to be very small.

The badge measured 50mm high by 36mm wide, was produced of bronze, and was worn on the left breast pocket of the uniform. A shield at the bottom, with dates ranging from 1919 to 1923, marked the member's entrance into the TeNo. It is

Obverse   **Reverse**

doubtful that a miniature of this award was produced. Certainly no miniature accompanied the award. The basic design of the badge centered about the red and black enamel membership insigne of the TeNo.

The award was presented in a hard presentation case, and was accompanied by an award document. The serial number of the award was engraved on the rear of the badge. Some specimens are found with the manufacturer's logo stamped on the pin shaft.

The exterior of the case is black and bears no markings. The interior of the lid is white satin, while the lower section is a cream-colored velvet.

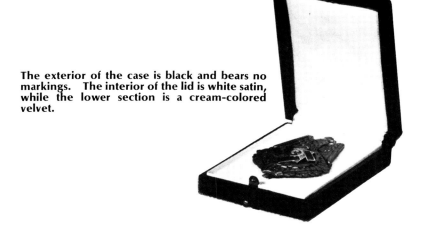

FAITHFUL SERVICE DECORATION
(Treudienst Ehrenzeichen)

As part of a continuing effort to exercise total control over the German people, and in order to obtain maximum effort from them, Hitler instituted a series of service awards that would serve as incentives. These awards were first mentioned in a Führer Decree of 14 November 1935. A few months later, the Reich Minister of the Interior initiated steps to establish such awards. A design created by Professor Richard Klein met with approval. On 30 January 1938, Hitler instituted five distinct service awards to recognize loyal service to the German people.

First among these awards was the Faithful Service Decoration (Treudienst Ehrenzeichen), which was awarded in recognition of loyal civilian service. It was created in three grades: 2nd Class in silver for 25 years service, 1st Class for 40 years service (identical in design to the 1st Class, but in gold), and a Special Grade (Sonderstufe), which was awarded for a total of 50 years of 'free market' service. A 10-year award was envisioned in the 1935 Decree, but never came into being.

The basic design of the three grades was identical - a 42mm cross with an oakleaf wreath suspended from a 35mm cornflower blue ribbon. On the center of the obverse of all three grades was a black enamel swastika. The upper arm of the Special

Obverse   Reverse

The 2nd Class award for 25 Years Loyal Service is in silver while the 1st Class award for 40 Years is in gold.   The suspension ribbon is cornflower blue.

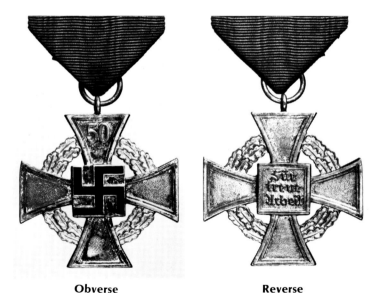

Obverse   Reverse

The Special Grade for 50 years of service with a private enterprise firm has the numeral '50' and the wreath in gold while the rest of the cross is silver.

Grade bore the numeral '50' in gold to denote 50 years of loyal work.   Additionally, the Special Class had a silver cross and gold oakleaves.   Neither the 2nd nor 1st Class bore a numeric designation as did the Special Class.   The square center shield on the reverse of the 2nd and 1st Classes bore the inscription "Für treue Dienste" (For

Loyal Service), while the Special Class was inscribed "Für treue Arbeit" (For Loyal Work).

Consideration of service time began when the prospective recipient reached the age of eighteen. Any break in service for duty with the military services (either active duty or as an administrator), with the Labor Service or with the police was counted towards the total time for loyal civil service. The recipient of the Special Grade was required to have 50 years of service (with recognized breaks in service as prescribed) with the same firm in free enterprise.

Christian Meyer became the first recipient of the 50 Year Faithful Service Cross when the medal was awarded personally by Adolf Hitler on 15 July 1938. The award was bestowed upon Herr Meyer for 50 years in the service of the Howaldtswerke.

The award was worn either on a medal bar above the left breast pocket, or on a ribbon bar, also above the left breast pocket. When worn as a ribbon, a miniature metal device corresponding to the grade of the award was affixed to the center. The decoration ranked with the other service awards below awards for military service. Only the highest class could be worn.

The award document that was rendered with the award did not refer to the Grade, but was instead a description, e.g., "As acknowledgment for 25 Years Loyal Service the Silver Faithful Service Decoration is awarded."

Recommendations for awards had to be forwarded through the Reich Minister of the Interior for interim approval to the President of the Reich Chancellery for final approval.

There is no accurate estimate of the numbers of each class awarded. However, a contract was let to a single firm in 1938 to produce 50,000 2nd Class awards. Certainly the Special Grade is rare considering the number of persons who would have qualified for it, and the publicity that each received upon being rendered the award.

2nd Class

1st Class   **Special Grade**

The case for the 2nd Class award is a red cardboard box with a burgundy inner lining. The lid has a '25' inside a spiked circle in silver. The hard cases of the 1st Class and Special Grade are identical, except for the '40' or '50' inside the gold wreath. The upper inside lid of the latter two grades is white satin, and sometimes bears the manufacturer's trademark.

Variation pattern award case for the Faithful Service Decoration. The cardboard box is black simulated leather with the silver 'LDO' proof on the upper lid. The lower section is recessed for the medal, and is off-white velvet.

Miniatures to exact scale.

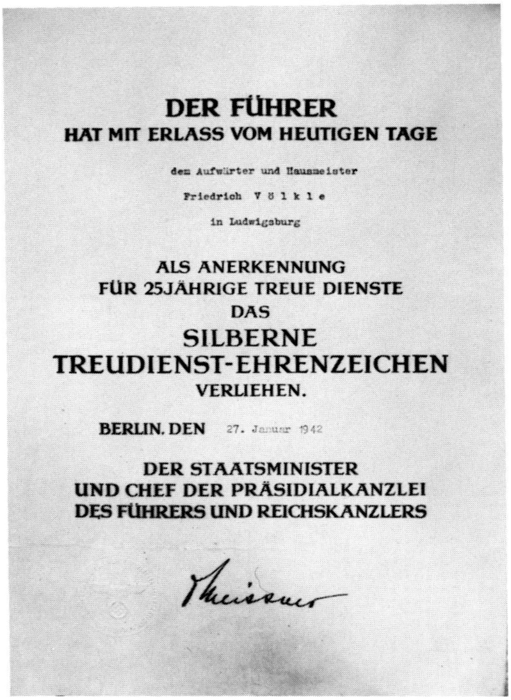

DER FÜHRER
HAT MIT ERLASS VOM HEUTIGEN TAGE

dem Aufwärter und Hausmeister

Friedrich V ö l k l e

in Ludwigsburg

ALS ANERKENNUNG
FÜR 25JÄHRIGE TREUE DIENSTE
DAS
SILBERNE
TREUDIENST-EHRENZEICHEN
VERLIEHEN.

BERLIN. DEN   27. Januar 1942

DER STAATSMINISTER
UND CHEF DER PRÄSIDIALKANZLEI
DES FÜHRERS UND REICHSKANZLERS

Bill Stump

Award document for the Faithful Service Decoration 2nd Class. Note that the document does not refer to the class of the award, but rather the number of years service and the fact that it is silver.

Jm Namen
des
Deutschen Volkes
verleihe ich

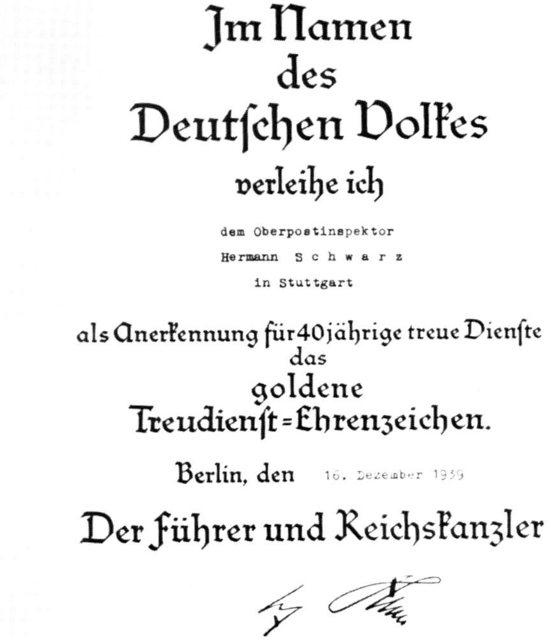

dem Oberpostinspektor

Hermann S c h w a r z

in Stuttgart

als Anerkennung für 40jährige treue Dienste
das
goldene
Treudienst=Ehrenzeichen.

Berlin, den   16. Dezember 1939

Der Führer und Reichskanzler

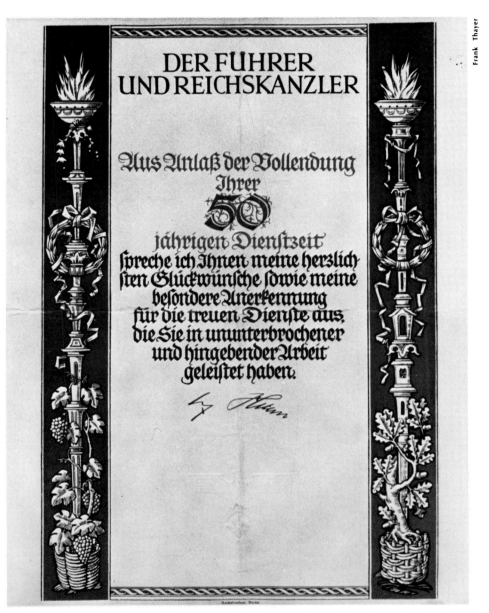

DER FÜHRER
UND REICHSKANZLER

Aus Anlaß der Vollendung
Ihrer
50
jährigen Dienstzeit
spreche ich Ihnen meine herzlich
sten Glückwünsche sowie meine
besondere Anerkennung
für die treuen Dienste aus,
die Sie in ununterbrochener
und hingebender Arbeit
geleistet haben.

Award document for 50 Years Faithful Service. Totally different in design than the two lesser awards, this document is brown down the sides, with red text in the first part of the text with the remainder done in black. The embossed national emblem in a wreath is below Hitler's signature.

Award document for the Faithful Service Decoration 1st Class. The Hitler signature is a facsimile. The embossed seal of the Orders Chancellery is at the lower left corner.

145

POLICE LONG SERVICE AWARDS
(Polizei-Dienstauszeichnung)

Professor Klein was also commissioned to design service awards for the active police.   The resulting medals were the second in a series of long service awards to be instituted on 30 January 1938 by order of the Führer.

The award was initially in three classes:

a.   3rd Class: A silver medal measuring 38mm, and suspended from a plain 35mm cornflower blue ribbon.   The obverse of the medal bore the police insigne, while the reverse had a large numeral '8' in the center (for 8 years of loyal service) surrounded by the inscription "Für treue Dienste in der Polizei".

Obverse   **Reverse**

b.   2nd Class: A silver 'Ordenskreuz' measuring 43mm, and suspended from a cornflower blue ribbon with a silver-gray woven police insigne.   The width of the ribbon ranged between 37mm and 51mm.   The obverse of the cross had a large police insigne, while the reverse bore the inscription "Für treue Dienste in der Polizei" in an oval shield.   It was awarded for 18 years service.

c.   1st Class: Identical in every respect to the 2nd Class, but finished in gold.   It was awarded for 25 years service.

The presentation case for the 3rd Class award is a cardboard box in green simulated leather. The lid has the numeral '8' surrounded by a silver spiked circle. The interior is burgundy flocking

An example of the 37mm ribbon is shown. However, ribbon widths ranged up to 51mm. It was not uncommon for the police emblem to be sewn to the ribbon rather than embroidered into the ribbon.

Obverse   Reverse

The cases for the 18 Year and 25 Year awards were identical. Both were normally hard cases of hinged construction with an exterior of green simulated leather. The numeral '18' or '25' surrounded by an oakleaf wreath was embossed on the top in either silver (18 years) or gold (25 years). The inside of the lid was finished in white satin, while the lower compartmented portion was finished in mouse-gray velvet. The ribbon in the illustration example is 51mm with the gold embroidered police emblem. A green presentation box identical to the 8 Year box is also known to have been used for the higher service crosses, but bearing the year designation of the higher awards.

Im Namen
des
Deutſchen Volkes
verleihe ich

als Anerkennung
für 25 jährige treue Dienſte in der Polizei
die
Polizei=Dienſtauszeichnung
erſter Stufe.

Berlin, den

Der Führer und Reichskanzler

Award Document for the Police Long Service Medal 1st Class.

Hauptmann Alois Tress poses in his police uniform prior to his entry into active military service.   Shown here as a Leutnant, he wears the silver 18 Year Police Long Service Award in parade form over his left breast pocket.   He went on to receive the gold 25 Year award.

Der Führer und Reichskanzler

hat mit Erlaß vom heutigen Tage

als Anerkennung
für 18jährige treue Dienste in der Polizei
die
Polizei = Dienstauszeichnung
zweiter Stufe
verliehen.

Berlin, den

Der Staatsminister
und Chef der Präsidialkanzlei
des Führers und Reichskanzlers

Police Long Service award 2nd Class for 18 Years Service. The 3rd Class award document for 8 Years Service is identical.

On the 12th of August, 1944, a still higher award was authorized to designate 40 years of loyal service. This was to be a metal device in gold with the numeral '40' with an oakleaf pattern affixed to the ribbon of the 1st Class award. No such device is known to this writer, and there is serious question as to whether or not the device was ever placed into production.

The award was worn either on the medal bar or in the form of a ribbon bar over the left breast pocket.   When worn as a ribbon bar, the 8 Year Service award was a plain cornflower blue ribbon, while the 18 Year Service had a silver police device and the 25 Year Service a gold device.   Normally, only the highest award could be worn at any given time, but if the recipient also held military long service awards, all police awards could be worn.   This award ranked below the military service awards in order of recognition.

In order to qualify for the award, a recipient had to be an active member of the police force or an administrator in the service of the police, and to have served loyally for the prescribed period.   Military service time was applied towards the total service period.   Following the annexation of Austria and Czechoslovakia in 1938 and 1939, police members of those countries were also eligible for the award.

It is possible that a ribbon device was also created for active police members who served in combat in a police formation.   This device was a police emblem in silver surmounting two crossed gold swords.

The award was rendered with a large award document.

LONG SERVICE AWARDS OF THE NATIONAL LABOR SERVICE
(Dienstauszeichnungen für den Reichsarbeitsdienst)

Third in the series of awards for recognition of loyal service to be instituted on 30 January 1938 were the Long Service Awards of the National Labor Service (Dienstauszeichnungen für den Reichsarbeitsdienst). This series of awards was designed and initially produced by Egon Jantke of Berlin.

The award came in four classes, but in two distinctive designs - one for men, and one for women.   Both designs were identical in size and shape (an oval measuring 40mm high and 33mm wide), and shared a common reverse motif - an oakleaf wreath around the outer edge with the inscription "Für treue Dienste im Reichsarbeitsdienst" (For Loyal Service in the National Labor Service).   The obverse of both had the oakleaf wreath border, but the similarity between the two ended there.   The men's award had the traditional National Labor Service (RAD) insigne: a spade with a swastika and two barley ears projected at an angle.   The women's bore the traditional young women's (weiblichen RAD or wJd) labor insignia: a swastika above two barley ears projected at an angle.   The awards came in four classes for both men and women:

a.   4th Class: A bronze medal suspended from a plain cornflower blue ribbon - for 4 Years Service.

b.   3rd Class: A silver medal suspended from a plain cornflower blue ribbon - for 12 Years Service.

Obverse of the Men's 4 Year Service award in bronze. This same design was carried out for all classes.

Obverse of the Women's 18 Year Service award with silver national emblem device. In the case of the 25 Year award, the medal and emblem would be gold.

The reverse of both the men's and women awards was identical.

c.   2nd Class: A silver medal suspended from a cornflower blue ribbon with a silver metal national emblem affixed to the ribbon, or a silver-gray national emblem embroidered into the ribbon - for 18 Years Service.

d.   1st Class: A gold medal suspended from a cornflower blue ribbon with a gilt metal national emblem affixed to the ribbon, or a gilt (yellow thread) national emblem embroidered into the ribbon - for 25 Years Service.

The silver and gold national emblem devices for 18 and 25 Years Service were established at the time of the creation of the RAD awards on 30 January 1938.[1]

Accumulation of service time was derived from honorable service with the RAD (or wJd), administrative service in support of the RAD in connection with the NSDAP, and military service time (which counted double) which might interrupt service with the RAD.   Conscripted labor service was not recognized as a basis for award, as the award was restricted to permanent staff members of the RAD.   Final approving authority for the award was vested in the Chancellery, with the recommendation coming from the Reichsarbeitsführer.

The medal was worn either on the medal bar or as a ribbon on the ribbon bar over the left breast pocket.   It ranked below military service awards and above state service awards in order of precedence.   It was most common for the women's award to be suspended from a bow ribbon rather than the straight suspension ribbon as found on the men's award.

When the award was worn in ribbon form, a miniature of the medal in gold was worn on the cornflower blue ribbon to designate the 1st Class award, and in silver to designate the 2nd Class award; no device was worn for either the 3rd or 4th Class awards. **Reichsarbeitsführer Hierl** issued an order on 2 August 1940 replacing this miniature with a metal device depicting a 9mm spade **and swastika,** with barley ears projecting at an angle from the spade's handle.   He quickly rescinded this order on 19 November 1940, and replaced this short-lived device with a metal national emblem (similar to, but smaller than, that used on the military long service awards.)   A gold eagle was affixed to the 1st Class ribbon, and a silver eagle was added to the 2nd Class ribbon.   No device was instituted for the 3rd or 4th Classes.

Alstott

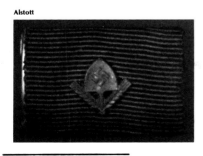

Short-lived RAD ribbon device introduced by Reichsarbeitsführer Hierl on 2 August 1940. This device lasted only three months before it was replaced by the national emblem device.

The RAD service ribbon was worn on a ribbon bar over the left breast pocket.

Presentation box for the 4 Year RAD Service award. The box is tan with the year designation in silver. The interior is tan, with the lower section compartmented to accommodate the medal.

Award Document for the 4th Class Medal.

Der Führer und Reichskanzler

hat mit Erlaß vom heutigen Tage

als Anerkennung für 4 jährige treue Dienstleistung
im Reichsarbeitsdienst
die
Dienstauszeichnung
für den Reichsarbeitsdienst
vierter Stufe
verliehen.

Berlin, den

Der Staatsminister
und Chef der Präsidialkanzlei
des Führers und Reichskanzlers

Im Namen
des
Deutschen Volkes
verleihe ich

als Anerkennung für 25 jährige treue Dienstleistung
im Reichsarbeitsdienst
die
Dienstauszeichnung
für den Reichsarbeitsdienst
erster Stufe.

Berlin, den

Der Führer und Reichskanzler

Award Document for the 1st Class Medal.

SS LONG SERVICE AWARDS
(SS-Dienstauszeichnungen)

The next service award to be founded on 30 January 1938 was the SS Long Service Award (SS-Dienstauszeichnungen) for members of the SS-Verfügungstruppen, SS-Totenkopfverbände, and the SS-Junkerschulen who were on active service, and had served honorably. All other SS members were only eligible to receive the NSDAP Long Service awards.

Four classes of the award were designed by Professor Karl Diebitsch of Munich as follows:

a. 4th Class: (4 Years Loyal Service) A black round medal measuring 38.5mm suspended from a 35mm plain cornflower blue ribbon. The obverse of the medal depicts the SS **Sigrunen** surrounded by an oakleaf wreath. The reverse shows a large numeral '4' with the inscription "Für treue Dienste in der SS" superimposed on it. This was the only class that was not authorized for award to officer personnel of the SS.

Obverse   **Reverse**
4th Class 4 Year Loyal Service Award

b. 3rd Class: (8 Years Loyal Service) A bronze round medal which measured 38mm and was suspended from a plain 35mm cornflower blue ribbon. It was awarded to all ranks. The obverse showed a large swastika with the SS **Sigrunen** surrounded by an oakleaf wreath superimposed in the center. The reverse bore a large numeral '8' with the inscription "Für treue Dienste in der SS" (For Loyal Service in the SS) superimposed on it.

Obverse   Reverse
3rd Class 8 Year Loyal Service Award

Shown here is an anomaly in the 8 Year SS Service medal. The medal at the right, shown to scale, is the standard pattern award. To the left is a medal measuring 42mm, but otherwise exact in detail. The only explanation that can be offered is that it was a manufacturer's design test strike. No other details are available.

    c. 2nd Class: (12 Years Loyal Service) This class was in the form of a 38mm swastika, to which an oakleaf wreath was affixed, surrounding the SS **Sigrunen** on the obverse. The reverse bore the inscription "Für treue Dienste in der SS". This silver award was suspended from a cornflower blue ribbon ranging from 35mm to 49mm with silver bullion SS **Sigrunen** embroidered in the center. It was awarded to all ranks.   157

d. 1st Class: (25 Years Loyal Service) This award was identical in every respect to the 12 Year award except that the award and the **Sigrunen** embroidered on the ribbon were gold. It was also awarded to all ranks.

Obverse
The design of the 2nd and 1st Class awards was identical. The finish of the SS Sigrunen of the 2nd Class was silver while the 1st Class was gold. The example shown here has the round suspension ring instead of the normal 'tear drop' suspension. The round suspension ring was an authorized manufacturer's variation.

The accumulation of service time could begin with the refounding of the NSDAP in 1925. The years 1925 to 1933, referred to as the 'Time of Struggle' or 'Kampfzeit', counted double, as did active military service. It is this double service time that would account for a 25 Year Service award. Recommendations for award came from the Reichsführer-SS, with the final approving authority vested in the Chancellery. The medal was presented with a large document certifying the award.

When the medal bar was not worn, a ribbon on a ribbon bar was worn over the left breast pocket. Only the highest class could be worn at one time unless the recipient held an award for military service. The 4th and 3rd Class awards on the ribbon bar were plain cornflower blue ribbons without a device, while the 2nd and 1st Class awards had silver and gold **Sigrunen** respectively.

158

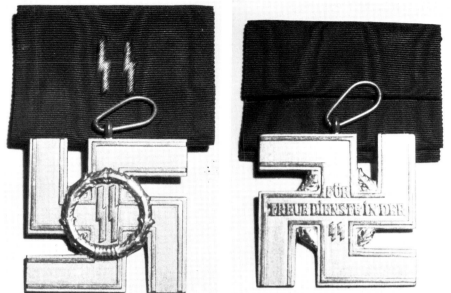

A Second Class Award with 'tear drop' suspension.

At this time it is appropriate to comment on the award's suspension ring. In most cases, the suspension was in the form of a closed 'tear drop', but there certainly were instances where the 2nd and 1st Class awards were produced with a circular ring (see pages 34/35, Orden und Ehrenzeichen im Dritten Reich , 1939 edition by Dr. Heinrich Doehle). Thus, this aspect alone cannot serve to differentiate between an original award and a reproduction.

The presentation case for the 4 Year Service Award is a black cardboard box with silver SS Sigrunen impressed on the lid. The interior is a mouse-gray flocking.

159

The presentation case for the 8 Year Service Award is a black simulated leather hard case with silver SS Sigrunen impressed in the lid. The inside of the lid is white satin, while the lower compartmented section is burgundy-colored. Award cases for the 2nd and 1st Classes are virtually identical, only slightly wider.

2nd Class presentation case. It can be assumed that the 1st Class case has the SS Sigrunen in gold since the 2nd Class is embossed in silver.

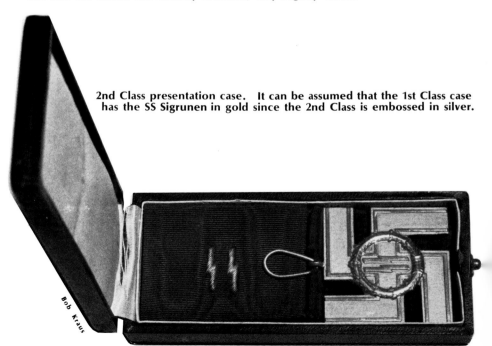

Bob Kraus

3rd Class Award Document for a member of a Death's Head Unit (Totenkopfverband).

Im Namen
des
Deutschen Volkes
verleihe ich

als Anerkennung für 8jährige treue Dienstleistung
in den SS-Totenkopfverbänden
die
SS-Dienstauszeichnung
dritter Stufe.
Berlin, den
Der Führer und Reichskanzler

Im Namen
des
Deutschen Volkes
verleihe ich

als Anerkennung für 25jährige treue Dienstleistung
in den SS-Verfügungstruppen
die
SS-Dienstauszeichnung
erster Stufe.
Berlin, den
Der Führer und Reichskanzler

1st Class Award Document for a member of the Verfügungs-truppe.

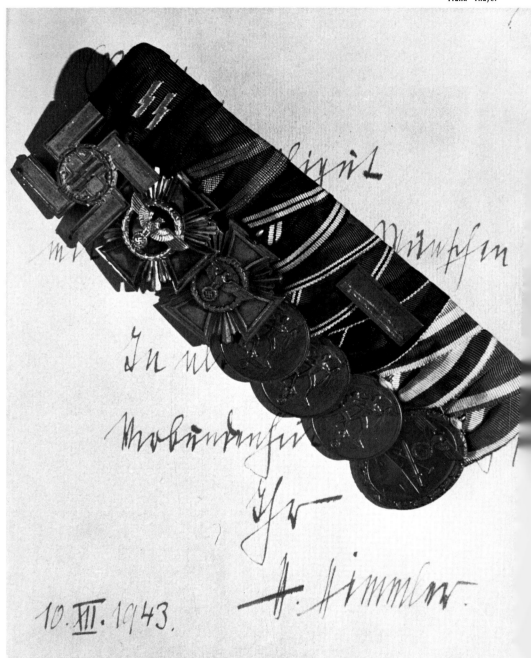

Frank Thayer

1. Medal bar belonging to Reichsführer-SS Heinrich Himmler consisting of the 12 Year SS Long Service, 15 Year NSDAP Long Service, 10 Year NSDAP Long Service, Occupation of Austria, Occupation of Czechoslovakia with 'Prague Castle' bar, Occupation of Memel, and West Wall medal.   The medal bar in the original presentation case was found on 2 May 1945 by men of Company E, 22nd Infantry Regiment, at Himmler's summer home at Gmund, Tergensee.

162

2.   Close-up of the 12 Year SS Long Service Cross.   Note that the wreath is an integral part of the cross stamping rather than being affixed to the surface of the cross as a separate piece.   Note also that the area between the wreath and the cross is solid.

3.   Medal bar in original presentation case.   Protective case may be more appropriate as it was probably constructed specifically for this bar when it was produced by the jeweller at Himmler's direction.   The case measures approximately 21cm x 15.5cm, is covered with a blue simulated leather, and is secured by two hinged clasps.   The interior of the lid is white satin bearing the logo 'T. Reimann Berlin W. Friedrichstr. 188'.   The bottom of the case is dark blue velvet, and is slotted to receive the medal bar and ribbon bar.

AIR RAID PROTECTION HONOR AWARD
(Luftschutz Ehrenzeichen)

Fifth among the honor awards instituted on the 30th of January, 1938, was the Air Raid Protection Honor Award (Luftschutz Ehrenzeichen) designed by Egon Jantke of Berlin. It came in two classes:

a.   2nd Class: This was awarded to persons who had served honorably in the civil defense of Germany since 30 January 1933, either in the National Air Raid Protection Service (Reichsluftschutzbund - RLB), the Civil Defense Volunteer. Service (Sicherheits-und Hilfsdienst), the Factory Police (Werkschutz), the Fire and Emergency Police, or the Ordinary Police.   It was necessary for members of the Ordnungspolizei to have accumulated at least four years' police service before they could be considered for the award.   The award was a 38-40mm round gray-colored medal suspended from a violet 31mm ribbon with black, red, and white edges.   The obverse showed a large swastika with the inscription 'Für Verdienste im Luftschutz' (For Service in the Luftschutz) surrounded by an oakleaf wreath.

Obverse   Reverse

2nd Class

b.   1st Class: This was awarded to persons who performed exceptional services in the civil defense of Germany.   The same persons eligible for the 2nd Class could qualify for the 1st Class.   The obverse of the gold cross had a swastika in the center encircled by the inscription 'Für Verdienste im Luftschutz', and suspended from a ribbon identical to that of the 2nd Class.   The cross measured 38.5-40mm.

The reverse of both classes bore the date '1938'.

The first awards of the 1st Class decoration were made on 20 April 1938.   Among the first recipients were Generalfeldmarschall Göring, General der Flieger Milch,

Obverse   **Reverse**
1st Class
Note the two variations in the manner of suspension.

Generalleutnant von Roques and Minister of the Interior Frick. This uncommon award was open to qualified male and female persons.

Unlike most other German awards, both classes of the award could be worn simultaneously, either on the medal bar or on a ribbon bar worn above the left breast

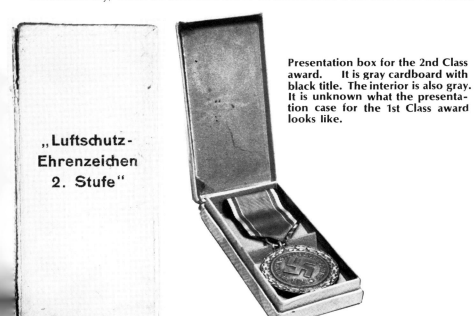

„Luftschutz-
Ehrenzeichen
2. Stufe"

Presentation box for the 2nd Class award. It is gray cardboard with black title. The interior is also gray. It is unknown what the presentation case for the 1st Class award looks like.

Presentation box to exact scale.

pocket.   An award of the 2nd Class was not a necessary prerequisite for an award of the 1st Class.

The medal was presented with a large award document upon recommendation by the Reichsminister der Luftfahrt and approved by the Chancellery.   Recommendations could only be submitted on 1 January, 1 April, 1 July and 1 October, each year.   Recommendations for the 2nd Class award were the responsibility of the Luftkreiskommandos, Industrial Reichsgruppe, and the President of the RLB.   Their recommendations had to be submitted by 1 March, 1 June, 1 September and 1 December.   After 4 May 1937 the award was open to foreign persons who had met the qualifications in the service of the German civil defense.

Early awards of the 1st Class were struck from bronze and the 2nd Class from aluminum, while later awards of both classes were produced from zinc.

Presentation envelope for the 2nd Class award.   The envelope is reddish-brown with black title.

DER FÜHRER
HAT MIT ERLASS VOM HEUTIGEN TAGE

dem Fahrer im Werkluftschutz

Emil   H e n n i n g e r

in Mannheim

IN ANERKENNUNG
SEINER VERDIENSTE IM LUFTSCHUTZ
DAS
LUFTSCHUTZ-EHRENZEICHEN
ZWEITER STUFE
VERLIEHEN.

BERLIN. den 30. September 1943

DER STAATSMINISTER UND CHEF
DER PRÄSIDIALKANZLEI

Meissner

Award document for the Air Raid Protection Honor Award 2nd Class.   Not shown in this photograph is the embossed eagle and swastika surrounded by an oakleaf wreath in the lower left hand corner.

FIRE BRIGADE DECORATION
(Feuerwehr Ehrenzeichen)

Two classes of the Fire Brigade decoration (Feuerwehr Ehrenzeichen) were instituted on 22 December 1936 by the Minister of the Interior. Both were designed by Herbert Knötel of Berlin, and were intended for award to both active and volunteer fire fighters and to fire administrators. The awards were as follows:

a. 2nd Class: A 43mm cross suspended from a red, white, and red ribbon with dark red edges. The center motif of the cross was a black swastika on a white field encircled by black. Projecting from the center and along the arms of the cross were red flames on a white field. Between the arms of the cross were the words "Für Verdienste im Feuerlöschwesen" (For Merit in the Fire Brigade Organization). All the metal portions were in silver. The reverse was plain; however, some manufacturers may have added their logo to the decoration. The 2nd Class was awarded for 25 years service, and was worn on the medal bar on the left breast.

b. 1st Class: This decoration was identical in description to the 2nd Class, except that it measured 58-60mm, and was a vaulted pinback badge worn on the lower left breast. This award was rendered for exceptionally meritorious service, including acts of bravery at fires.

1936 pattern Fire Brigade decoration 1st Class. A pinback award, all metal portions were silver.

Silver with Variation Suspension Loop.

Recommendations for award came from the Reichsführer-SS (in his capacity as Chief of the German Police, which controlled the fire departments), and were approved by the Minister of the Interior. Hitler retained the right to sign the award documents of the 1st Class decoration, with the signing authority for the 2nd Class being delegated to Reich Minister Meissner. A 1st Class award was automatically forthcoming for a fireman killed in the line of duty.

The decree of 30 January 1938 which created a series of service awards also served to change the Fire Brigade decoration. The pin-back version was eliminated altogether. The 2nd Class remained unchanged, but the 1st Class now took on the form of the 2nd Class, with all metal portions being finished in gold. The suspension ribbon for both classes was identical. The criteria and recommendation procedure remained unchanged. However, after the outbreak of the war, non-Germans in the service of the fire department were also qualified for the award. An order dated 12 August 1944 instituted a 40-year service device - a gold metal device with a '40' surrounded by a oakleaf wreath. While it is possible that such devices were placed into production, it is not known if they were actually bestowed.

It should be noted that the more common pattern of the 2nd Class decoration has a ball-like suspension loop through which the suspension ring passes.

Gold with Standard Suspension Loop.

The 1936 pattern 2nd Class award became the basic design for the 1938 1st and 2nd Class awards. The 1st Class was finished in gold while the 2nd Class was silver.

The presentation case for the Fire Brigade decoration is a hinged, hard case with an exterior of black simulated leather, and bears no lid designation. The upper interior is white satin void of any designation, and the lower portion is black velvet recessed to accommodate the cross.

MINE RESCUE SERVICE DECORATION
(Grubenwehr-Ehrenzeichen)

The last award covered in the decree of 30 January 1938 was the Mine Rescue Service decoration. This decoration was not being founded, but (like the Fire Brigade decoration) was being redesigned.

The first pattern award had been instituted on 13 November 1936 in recognition of the following:

    a.   15 years service as a member of the Mine Rescue Service.

    b.   For less than 15 years service if a member of the Mine Rescue Service was injured in the line of duty.

It was also awarded to:

    a.   Members of the Mine Rescue Service who performed outstanding service, particularly at the risk of their lives.

    b.   Non-members who rendered outstanding service in conjunction with the Mine Rescue Service.

    c.   Non-members who risked their lives in life-saving operations during a mine disaster.

169

The 50mm round breast badge was designed by Professor Schweitzer. The medal's center motif was a crossed miner's hammer and pick with the national emblem superimposed. Around the outer edge was the inscription 'Für Verdienste um das Grubenwehrwesen' (For Merit in the Mine Rescue Service). The award gave the appearance of old silver, and was usually produced from aluminum.

Obverse   **Reverse**

The presentation case is black with gold embossed emblem on the lid. The interior lid is white satin while the lower section is dark blue velvet.

The first pattern gave way to a second design, which was also designed by Professor Schweitzer.   This was a 35mm silver medal suspended from a 30mm ribbon of yellow and black with white edges.   The obverse of the medal kept the crossed miner's hammer and pick with the national emblem superimposed.   The reverse bore the inscription 'Für Verdienste im Grubenwehrwesen', with an oakleaf wreath partially surrounding it.

Obverse   **Reverse**

The medal was presented with an award document, and was worn on the medal or ribbon bar above the left breast pocket.   The criteria for award were modified as well - now the badge was restricted solely to members of the Mine Rescue Service.

CUSTOMS SERVICE DECORATION
(Zollgrenzschutz-Ehrenzeichen)

Following a Führer-order of 17 February 1939, the Reich Minister for Finance was authorized to award the newly instituted Customs Service decoration for loyal service.   While only a single medal was awarded, it was recognized that it was awarded in two degrees - one for the clerks of the Customs Service, and the other for high administrative officials and uniformed Customs officials performing border duty.   Four years of service were required for the uniformed official to be eligible, while eight years were the requisite for civilians performing civil service functions in connection with the Customs Service.   The award could also be rendered for especially meritorious service in connection with the Customs Service.

Obverse   **Reverse**

**Customs Award with Miniature
Insigne on Ribbon.**

The award took the shape of a bronze 'Ordenskreuz' suspended from a cornflower blue ribbon. The cross measured 42mm and had the national emblem partially encircled by an acanthus wreath on the obverse, with the inscription 'Für treue Dienste im Zollgrenzschutz' (For Loyal Service in the Customs Service) encircled in a wreath on the reverse. The suspension ribbon, which measured 35-50mm, bore a Customs insigne embroidered in yellow thread or a bronze metal insigne device affixed to the ribbon. When only the ribbon was worn, a miniature Customs insigne was worn on it. It was worn either on the medal bar or on a ribbon bar over the left breast pocket. It ranked below the military service awards.

Der Führer
hat mit Erlaß vom heutigen Tage

für treue Dienste im Zollgrenzschutz
das
Zollgrenzschutz-Ehrenzeichen
verliehen.

Berlin, den

Der Staatsminifter
und Chef der Präsidialkanzlei
des Führers und Reichskanzlers

Award Document for the Customs Decoration.

SERVICE BADGE FOR GERMAN FEMALE RAILWAY STAFF
(Dienstnadel für Eisenbahnerinnen)

Dr. Julius Dorpmüller, Reich Minister of Transportation, instituted a service badge for female staff members of the German Railway System who occupied positions normally held by male workers.   It was established in 1944 in the following grades:

a.   Gold: 10 years active service

b.   Silver: 6 years active service

c.   Bronze: 3 years active service

The first awards were presented by State Secretary Dr. Ganzenmüller in October 1944 to 30 female recipients who had earned the bronze and silver awards.   It is doubtful that anyone qualified for the award in gold before the war came to an end.

First awarding of the Service Badge for Female Railway members on 13 October 1944.

B. Regnemer

Obverse   **Reverse**

The service badge took the form of a winged railway wheel surrounded by laurel leaves with a swastika at the top.   It measured only 30mm by 22mm, and was worn as a brooch on the upper left side of the jacket.   Pieces observed had a plain reverse with horizontal clasp.

Due to the late date of introduction and the limited number of persons who would qualify for such an award, this service badge is considered to be quite rare.

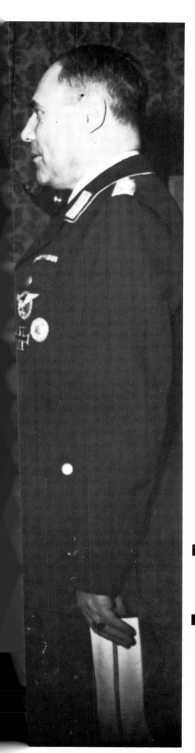

Hitler presents Generalleutnant Bodenschatz with the Golden Party Badge on his 50th birthday, 11 December 1940.

NSDAP Awards

GOLDEN PARTY BADGE
(Goldenes Parteiabzeichen)

An order dated 13 October 1933 and signed by Hitler decreed that all persons who had had uninterrupted service in the NSDAP since 27 February 1925, and who held NSDAP membership numbers 1 to 100,000, would be awarded the newly instituted Golden Party badge on 9 November 1933.   Party membership had reached 700,000 by 30 January 1933, and had already surpassed the 100,000 mark by September 1930.[1]   Of the 100,000 persons who might have been qualified, the restrictions of active and unbroken membership reduced the number of awards to 22,282 - 20,487 to men and 1,-795 to women.

The badge was identical to the basic NSDAP membership pin, with the addition of a gold oakleaf wreath surrounding it.   The Party number of the recipient was engraved on the reverse.

A 30.5mm badge was worn on the military or political uniform, while a smaller version measuring 25mm was worn with civilian clothes.   Regulations prescribed that the large badge should be worn next to or above the Iron Cross 1st Class, or, when worn on the tie, must be in line with the buttons of the two breast pockets.   The smaller version was worn on the tie or lapel.   Persons holding the Golden Party Badge wore this in lieu of the standard pattern membership pin.

25mm Badge   **30.5mm Badge**

---

[1]*NSDAP Partei-Statistik 1935, Vol. 1 (Also includes exact breakdown of the Golden Party Badges awarded by location, percentile, sex, etc.) Also see Der Schulungsbrief, No. 8/9, 1938, for a similar article.*

Two pattern reverses of the 30.5mm badge.

Reverse of the 25mm badge. This particular example is an uncommon screw-back version worn in the buttonhole of the lapel. Standard patterns had the horizontal pin. Note the bearer's Party number.

Hoover Institution

Franz Xaver Schwarz is shown wearing the 25mm badge on the lapel of his civilian suit.

An identical badge was awarded ceremoniously each year on the 30th of January to persons who had demonstrated outstanding service to the Party or State. Hitler and other high ranking Party members undoubtedly used this honorary award from time to time as a means to achieve a special end. The obverse of the badge was identical to that awarded to veteran Party members, while the reverse bore the initials 'A.H.' and the date of the award. This award was presented with a very large award document printed in gold.

179

Dr. Robert Ley extends his birthday greeting to Reichsmarschall Göring. Note the Golden Party Badge being worn on the pocket flap at the right. This was often done, but contrary to the prescribed manner as depicted by Ley.

The presentation case for the standard pattern Golden Party Badge is a hinged hard case with black simulated leather exterior. The upper inside section is white satin, while the lower section is black velvet. The case for the achievement or service version is virtually identical except that the area in the center is recessed to receive the badge and clasp. The latter case has a spring-tension release catch. There is no lid designation on either case.

Reverse of the Golden Party Badge awarded for outstanding service. Since it was awarded on 30 January of each year, only the year date will change from badge to badge.

Glenn Browning

The large and small size Honorary Golden Party Badges presented to von Brauchitsch differed from the standard Honorary badges in that these were presented in March rather than 30 January (for the successful occupation of Prague), and bore Hitler's full signature rather than the initials.

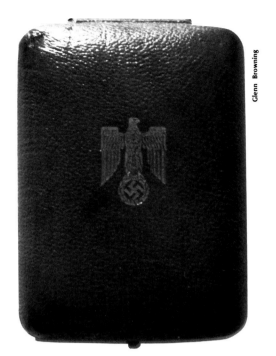

Set of Golden Party Badges honorarily awarded by Hitler to the Chief of the Army, Walter von Brauchitsch. The presentation case is dome-shaped, covered with red Morocco leather with a gold national emblem on the lid, and a gold border around the top and bottom edge of the case. The case measures 67mm x 90mm. It opens by means of a spring-tension release. The interior of the top is white silk, and the compartmented bottom is white velvet.

The few Old Guard Party members who received the award were given special considerations within and outside the Party. The Golden Party badge was prominently worn on every possible occasion.

The last award to be made of the Golden Party Badge was on 27 April 1945 when Hitler removed his own Golden Party Badge Number 1 from his uniform, and presented it to Frau Goebbels before the assembled inner circle of Nazis and generals in the Berlin bunker.[2]

It is a common misconception that Hitler held Party number 7 - he didn't. After the refounding and reorganization of the NSDAP he took Party number 1. He also held SA and NSKK membership Number 1. Nazi propagandists liked to call him Party Comrade 7, but this only refers to events before November 9, 1923 - when he, in fact, held Party Number 55 (he was the 7th member of the Party's Central Committee in 1919 and 1920, which is where this legend originated).[3]

---

[2] *Technically, this award should be seen as a personal tribute to Frau Goebbels rather than as a bestowal of the badge. Magda Goebbels was an old Party member, and presumably possessed her own Golden Badge.*

[3] *Frau Hess alleges that she was personally presented the Führer's Golden Party badge during a state function in the late 30's. The significant point of this is that Frau*

Variation Oakleaf patterns showing pointed and rounded leaves.

Award certificate for Golden Party Badge Number 81882 awarded on 8 June 1944 to Franz Hobart. Hobart joined the NSDAP in November 1927 and was awarded a Party number in the 60,000 series. He was called to military duty in 1928 and allowed his membership to lapse. He rejoined the Party in 1931 and received a new Party number, 783,576. In 1942 Hobart applied for his old Party number but was informed that it was no longer available. On 8 June 1944, however, he was given Party number 81,882 with retroactive membership from 20 January 1928. For a fee of RM 2.50 he was able to acquire his Golden Party Badge.

Hess states that the award bore serial number 1, and not number 7. She was very emphatic about the serial number designation. She alleges that the award was destroyed in a fire.

184

IN WÜRDIGUNG
SEINER VERDIENSTE UM VOLK
UND REICH VERLEIHE ICH
HERRN PROFESSOR
FRIEDRICH FRANZMANN
DAS GOLDENE EHRENZEICHEN
DER
N · S · D · A · P

MÜNCHEN · DEN 30. JANUAR 1938.

DER FÜHRER:

Berichtigungsabzug 17. 4. 39

Award document for the Special Class of the Golden Party Award. This very large parchment document has the national emblem and designation of the award finished in gold.

GAU MUNICH COMMEMORATIVE BADGE OF 9 NOVEMBER 1923
(Gau München Erinnerungsabzeichen des 9 Nov. 1923)

A 35mm bronze badge was created to commemorate the Munich 'Putsch' of 9 November 1923, and was awarded by the Munich Gau of the NSDAP. Established in 1933, the badge consisted of a swastika bearing the date '1933', encircled by a round oakleaf wreath with the words "Und ihr habt doch gesiegt" (And yet you have conquered) - a slogan which was later used on the Blood Order, which replaced this award. While in existence, it was worn on the left breast.

This badge never received official recognition as a national award, and is included here only because it is so closely related to the Blood Order.

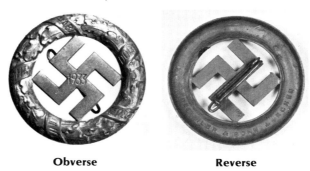

Obverse   Reverse

DECORATION OF 9 NOVEMBER 1923 - BLOOD ORDER
(Ehrenzeichen vom 9. November 1923-Blutorden)

In March 1934 Hitler instituted the 'Decoration of 9 November 1923' to commemorate the abortive march of 9 November 1923 during which he and a group of followers attempted to seize power from the Bavarian Government in Munich. This was a national Order honoring the Party comrades killed in the uprising. This gave rise to its more popular designation 'Blood Order'.

In order to be eligible for the award, persons who had participated in the events of 9 November 1923 had to be a member of the Party or one of its formations by January 1, 1932, and this membership had to be continuous. If a holder of the Blood Order left the Party he had to relinquish his award.

On May 30, 1938, the conditions for award of the Order were considerably expanded, much to the dismay of the 'Old Fighters'. Now the award could be bestowed on persons who had rendered outstanding services to the Party in the 'Kampfzeit'. These services were as follows:

(1) To have received a death sentence which was later commuted to life imprisonment.

(2)   To have served at least a one-year jail sentence for political crimes.

(3)   To have been severely wounded.

Thus, someone like Martin Bormann, not a Party member in 1923, could receive the award, which he wore prominently, under qualification (2), while such key people as Goebbels and Lutze, who certainly performed outstanding services to the Party, could not.

All Party members who lost their lives in the service of the Party were automatically awarded the Blood Order; this practice, which was retroactive to 1923, ceased in 1942, the last award going to Reinhard Heydrich.

At least two women were awarded the Blood Order - Sister Pia of Munich, who had participated in the march of November 9, and Katharina Grünewald, killed in the service of the Party in 1929, who received it posthumously.

Sister Pia joins her comrades in the historical beer hall 'Bürgerbräukeller' for a reunion of Old Guard Party members who made the 9 November 1923 Putsch march with Hitler.   Sister Pia, who is still alive, was awarded Blood Order Nr. 25.

The Blood Order was carefully scrutinized by the Office of the 9th of November, a body set up under the leadership of Christian Weber of Munich to look after the participants of the Putsch.

The design was the creation of jeweller Josef Fuess of Munich, while the medal was struck by the firm of E. Schmidhäussler in Pforzheim.   The initial order by the NSDAP numbered 50,000 copies, but after Fuess had delivered 20,000 Blood Orders, the order was cancelled. During the course of the twelve year Reich, two distinct design variants emerged:

a. 1st Pattern: A 40mm round genuine silver medal suspended from a red ribbon with white and black striped edges. The obverse design depicted an eagle clutching an oakleaf wreath inside of which was the date '9.NOV.'. To the right of the eagle was the inscription 'MÜNCHEN 1923-1933'. The major characteristic of the obverse of the first pattern was the exceptionally long down-turned portion of the eagle's beak. The reverse depicted the Feldherrnhalle Monument over which was a swastika with rays emanating from it. Arched above the swastika was the motto "UND IHR HABT DOCH GESIEGT" (And yet you have conquered). Below the monument was the silver content designation (990/1000) and the jeweller's logo 'J. Fuess München'. The serial number of the award (not the recipient's Party number) was engraved immediately below the steps of the monument.

Obverse

Bob Kraus

Reverse

While there is little to distinguish between the front of a 1st or 2nd Pattern Blood Order, there is an obvious way to distinguish the two from the reverse. The 1st Pattern has the manufacturer's logo arched above the rim at the bottom of the medal. This logo reads 'J. Fuess München' in block capital letters.

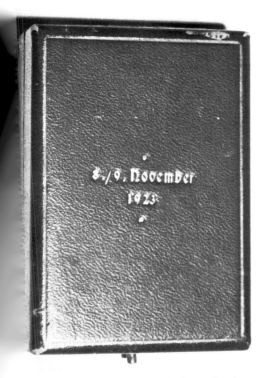

Note the numbered label on the bottom of the presentation case. Its number matches that of the Blood Order it contains (number 1002). See medal at left. The case is covered with smooth-grained maroon leather with the inscription in gold. The upper inside lid is in white satin while the lower interior is in white velvet.

b. 2nd Pattern: This pattern emerged sometime in 1938. Its production was rigidly controlled by the RZM, but the exact number produced is not known. The basic design remained unchanged, but the manufacturer's logo was removed from the reverse. Additionally, the silver quality limits were reduced so that a designation of 800/1000 was possible. This pattern measured 40.5mm in diameter and was 2.1mm thick.

Obverse　　　　　**Reverse**

The suspension ribbon for this particular specimen is rather unique in that it appears that the Order could be removed from the ribbon, allowing the ribbon to remain on the uniform as prescribed by regulations. The serial number of this particular Order is 3750, indicating that this was probably an honor award.

Party regulations prescribed in detail the manner in which the Order was to be worn. When worn on the 'brown shirt' or service jacket, it was worn on the right pocket in two parts. A length of ribbon in the shape of a pie wedge was affixed to the pocket flap. The Order was then either pinned under the pocket flap, or the suspension ribbon (altered to have a button hole) was placed over the pocket button, with the flap then being buttoned. When the Order was removed from the pocket, the rosette remained on the pocket flap. Uniforms not having a breast pocket were authorized to have the Blood Order ribbon worn through the second buttonhole (as with the Iron Cross 2nd Class, etc.).   Initial regulations prohibited wear on the Air Force flying jacket.   However, a pin-back rosette was introduced in September 1941, and was authorized to be worn on the Flying Jacket and other uniform jackets without pockets.

Interestingly enough, early regulations referred to the Decoration of 9 November 1923 as being the ribbon worn in the buttonhole of the right breast pocket, and make no mention of the medal - "The decoration is a red, black-white striped ribbon worn in the buttonhole of the right breast pocket of the brown-shirt or service tunic."[4]

Besitzurkunde,   the official record of award carried by the recipient.   This award was rendered on 31 October 1941 indicating a probable Honor Award of the Blood Order.   The number of the award was entered on the document and engraved below the Feldherrnhalle Monument on the reverse of the Order.

[4]*Verordnungsblatt der SA, Nr. 18, 15/3/34.*

The award was presented in a hard red case with the inscription '8./9. November 1923' in gold on the lid. In addition, most recipients were given a certificate of ownership, or Besitzurkunde. On the front of this red linen document was a facsimile of the obverse of the Order and the title 'Besitzurkunde für den Blutorden der NSDAP'. The actual award document was rather large, and was presented in a red leather covered document binder.

The actual number of awards that were presented has not yet been determined, but considering the number of men that made the original march, the 436 posthumous awards, and the awards for outstanding service, it is likely that the figure would number under 6,000.

The award document for the Blood Order presented an an Honor Award, presented to Party Member Friedrich Knill on 31 May 1940. The facsimile of the Blood Order on the document is in relief. This ornate document was encased in a large red leather binder.

GOLDEN HITLER YOUTH HONOR BADGE
(Goldenes Hitler-Jugend Ehrenabzeichen)

The Golden Hitler Youth Honor Badge (Goldenes Hitler-Jugend Ehrenzeichen), basically an extension of the Hitler Youth Membership pin designed by Reichs-jugendführer Baldur von Schirach, was instituted as a national award by von Schirach on 23 June 1934. It is possible that the award had been in existence since 1933, but without the national recognition now afforded it.

The diamond-shaped pin measuring 17mm by 28.5mm was the usual Hitler Youth pin (a black enamel swastika overlapping a red and white enamel field), but with a gold background (instead of the normal silver) and gold border. It was intended to be awarded to Hitler Youth members, both male and female, who had been members prior to the Youth Rally at Potsdam on 2 October 1932. An estimated 107,000 persons were members as of this time, and would have been eligible for the badge, providing they had accumulated five years of uninterrupted service in the Hitler Youth. This latter condition was expanded to include service in other Nazi organizations. The

Temporary Award Document for the Golden Hitler Youth Honor Badge. Award Number 102995 was presented for continuous HJ membership since 1931. Note the title of the award, 'HJ Ehrenzeichens' (Hitler Youth Honor Badge.)

Karl-Heinz Ziegelmaier, who served on the 'Pocket' Battleship Tirpitz, wears the Golden Hitler Youth Honor badge along with his military decorations.

foundation decree also prescribed that the badge could be awarded for merit without regard to length of service.

The badge was awarded with a notification of award, and was worn on the left breast pocket (left lapel for girls) in lieu of the Hitler Youth membership pin.

In addition to the RZM logo, the serial number of the award was placed on the reverse of the badge.

Obverse   **Reverse**

C. Hannahs

GOLDEN HITLER YOUTH HONOR BADGE WITH OAKLEAVES
(Goldenes Hitler-Jugend Ehrenzeichen mit Eichenlaub)

The addition of a golden oakleaf border in lieu of the plain golden border was made the year following the introduction of the Golden Hitler Youth Decoration (as it was sometimes called) in 1934. Slightly larger in size - 19.5mm by 32.5mm - it was intended as an award for merit. It was bestowed upon members of the Hitler Youth and also on non-members who had made a significant contribution to the advancement of the Hitler Youth. It was also awarded by von Schirach to notable non-Germans, and was one of the few national orders that could be bestowed by someone other than the Führer.

An estimated 250 awards were rendered making this one of the rarest national awards. Some notable recipients of the award were Heinrich Himmler, Albert Speer, and Dr. Robert Ley.

It was worn on the left breast pocket. Presentation was made with an award document personally signed by Baldur von Schirach.

Obverse

Reverse
(Not to scale)

Reichsjugendführer Baldur von Schirach, shown here in army uniform, wears the Golden Hitler Youth Honor Badge with Oakleaves over the Golden Party Badge, indicating the relative merit of the two.

GOLDEN HITLER YOUTH HONOR BADGE WITH OAK LEAVES, SPECIAL CLASS
(Goldenes HJ Ehrenzeichen mit Eichenlaub, Sonderstufe)

In 1942, on the occasion of the 35th birthday of Baldur von Schirach, the leadership of the Hitler Youth was in a bit of a quandary as to what to present to their former leader for a birthday gift. A special award was finally decided on - a special grade of the Golden Hitler Youth Honor badge with Oakleaves. This was to be a one-time award to recognize the achievements of von Schirach on the advancement of the Hitler Youth, and to commemorate his 35th birthday.

The commission for the badge went to the Munich jeweller, Peter Rath, who had been designated 'Hofjuwelier' (the equivalent of Court Jeweller). The resulting award was basically a replica of the Golden HJ badge, but all similarity ended there. The Hitler Youth emblem had a black enamel swastika with a silver background, and was accentuated by small diamonds and rubies. The oakleaf border was hand tooled in genuine gold.

Satisfied with Rath's results, the leadership of the HJ presented the badge to von Schirach on 9 May 1942.

B. Swearingen

(Not to scale)

Golden Hitler Youth Honor Badge with Oakleaves, Special Class

COBURG BADGE
(Coburger Abzeichen)

The Coburg Badge (Coburger Abzeichen) was instituted by Hitler on 14 October 1932, just ten years after the Nazi triumph over the Communists in Coburg.

A patriotic weekend rally was held in Coburg on 14/15 October 1922, and an invitation to attend was extended to Hitler and some of his associates in the young Nazi Party. Hitler mustered 800 SA men, including a band, and traveled by rail from Munich to Coburg in the first of many Nazi 'expeditions'. Once at the rally, there were numerous clashes between the Nazis and the Communists in the streets; the final result was a victory for Hitler and his Party. Party annals refer to the event at Coburg as the 'Deutscher Tag in Coburg' (German Day in Coburg). The badge was declared an official Party and national decoration in a decree signed by Hitler on 6 November 1936.

The badge, largely designed by Hitler himself, came only in bronze,[5] and measured 40mm wide by 54mm high. It was worn on the left breast. It featured a sword, point downward, in a vertical position over a swastika in an oval. At the top of the badge was the Coburg Castle. The outer edge of the oval was a laurel wreath. Inside the laurel wreath was the inscription 'Mit Hitler in Coburg 1922-1932' (With Hitler in Coburg 1922-1932). The original badge was made of massive bronze and was slightly convex, while later versions were thinner and flat.

Only 436 names were entered on the official Party award list as recipients.

Obverse

B. Regnemer

Reverse

---

[5] *A variation exists in dull silver with red enamel swastika, but this was probably a private purchase badge and not officially sanctioned.*

In the year following the introduction of the Coburg Badge, Hitler and his lieutenants review the passing of Nazi Party formations, probably at the Reichsparteitag in Nürnberg. The Coburg Badge, being the earlier instituted, is worn above the Saxony (et al.) badge.

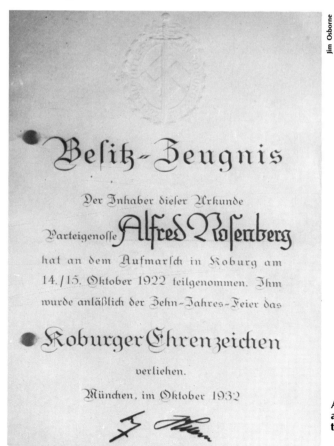

Besitz-Zeugnis

Der Inhaber dieser Urkunde

Parteigenosse **Alfred Rosenberg**

hat an dem Aufmarsch in Koburg am 14./15. Oktober 1922 teilgenommen. Ihm wurde anläßlich der Zehn-Jahres-Feier das

Koburger Ehrenzeichen

verliehen.

München, im Oktober 1932

Alfred Rosenberg's award document for the Coburg Badge.

NÜRNBERG PARTY DAY BADGE OF 1929
(Nürnberger Parteitagsabzeichen 1929)

A badge was established on 15 August 1929 by the commander of the SA in commemoration of the 4th Party Rally held at Nürnberg on 1/4 August 1929. It was worn continuously thereafter as an honor badge, and was officially recognized as such in a Führer decree of 6 November 1936. All NSDAP members who had attended the rally were entitled to wear the badge.

The badge measured 21mm wide by 48mm high, and was worn on the left breast. It featured the Nürnberg Castle above the word 'NÜRNBERG' at the top, with an eagle astride a helmet in the center, surrounded by the wording '1914-1919 NSDAP Parteitag 1929'. The badge was produced in gray, silver and gold, with no

Obverse

Adolf Bökenkrüger

Reverse

199

significance being attributed to the color differences. The most common was the gray version, either solid or hollow-backed.

An estimated 60,000 persons would have qualified for the badge.

Additionally, there was a cased, non-portable award measuring 35mm wide by 80mm high, produced in bronze, silver or gold. The precise conditions for award are not known, but it is thought to be an award for events held during the rally.

Bob Kraus

The cased award was in bronze, silver or gold. The reverse bore the manufacturer's (and probably the designer's) logo.

Nürnberg Party Day Badge of 1929 - Non-Portable Version.

Case for the Non-Portable Award. It is covered with smooth-grained, maroon leather with the upper interior lid in white satin and the lower interior portion in gray-green velvet.

BADGE OF THE SA RALLY AT BRUNSWICK 1931
(Abzeichen des SA-Treffens Braunschweig 1931)

The third badge to gain official recognition on 6 November 1936 as a national award of the NSDAP was the badge of the SA Rally at Brunswick in 1931 (Abzeichen des SA-Treffens Braunschweig 1931). It was initially struck as a badge to commemorate the rally of slightly more than 100,000 SA and SS members at Brunswick on 17/18 October 1931. SA-Gruppe Nord, which hosted the rally under the leadership of SA-Gruppenführer Viktor Lutze, played the principal role at the rally. It was at this assembly, which followed closely on the heels of the Stennes putsch, that Hitler gained the assurance of the SA rank and file and at which Lutze gained a reputation as a totally loyal Party member. Hitler did not forget this act of loyalty in 1934 when he named Lutze to replace the executed Röhm. It was at this meeting also that Hitler authorized the creation of 24 new Standarten, thus expanding the SA, and recognized the Motor-SA and NSKK.

All Party members who had officially attended the rally were authorized to wear the badge on their left breast. SA officers from the rank of SA-Standartenführer upwards had the authority to make an official entry confirming award in the member's Party book.

Two variations of the badge existed - the first probably the original rally badge, and the second the badge produced following the Hitler decree of 1936.

a. 1st Pattern: An early style Party eagle at the top of an oval badge with an oakleaf wreath around the outer edge. Within the wreath was the inscription 'SA-Treffen Brunswick 17/18 Oktober 1931' (SA Rally Braunschweig 17/18 October 1931). At the bottom of the wreath was a bow. This badge measured 37mm wide by 50mm high.

1st Pattern

2nd Pattern

b. 2nd Pattern: Same basic design as the 1st Pattern except that it was 37mm wide and 52mm high.

Some of the very early original rally badges were stamped tin, and measured as much as 47mm wide.

This badge is found with the stamped out as well as the solid back. In the case of the solid back badge, it bore the inscription 'RZM M1/17 Ges./Gesch'. The badge ranges from 'silver' for the early patterns to gray for the later pattern.

This SS officer in 1933 wore the 1931 Braunschweig SA Rally badge as a NSDAP Honor badge before it had been officially designated as such.

FRONTBANN BADGE
(Frontbannabzeichen)

The Frontbann badge was instituted in 1932 by the SA-Gruppe Berlin-Brandenburg. The Frontbann was set up in 1924 as a substitute for the then banned SA. The badge was awarded to men who had joined the Frontbann before 31 December 1927, or who had held simultaneous membership in the NSDAP and one of the many uniformed right-wing formations prior to that date. The badge was designated an official decoration of the NSDAP in 1933.

The silver badge, which measured approximately 20mm, consisted of a swastika with a helmet in the center. On the arms of the swastika was the motto "WIR-WOLLEN-FREI-WERDEN" (We want to be free). The reverse of the badge had a pin, a number, and, in some cases, the RZM designation. The badge was worn on the left breast pocket.

The badge was no longer authorized for wear by the end of 1934.

Obverse   Reverse

Emil Behrendt might be considered typical of the early Party leaders who earned their awards as members of the Old Guard. After being released from service as an Infantryman at the end of World War I, Behrendt returned to civilian life only to volunteer for the Freikorps under General von Oven. He participated in action against the Poles near Posen in early 1919. After being absorbed into the Reinhardt Brigade, he took part in quelling the riots by the communists. After the failure of the Kapp Putsch, Behrendt found himself out of work, and was forced to perform voluntary help on farms. He was an early follower of Hitler, which caused him to join the SA and then the NSDAP. In 1933 he was accepted into the SS, and given the simultaneous position of Block Leader on active service with the Party. By 1935 he was promoted to the rank of Ortsgruppenleiter. His long and continuous service to the Party earned him the Golden Party Badge, the Frontbann Badge, the Nürnberg Party Day Badge, and the 10 and 15 Year NSDAP Long Service awards.

PARTY DISTRICT COMMEMORATIVE BADGES
(Traditions-Gau-Abzeichen)

The right to award the Gau commemorative badges was vested in the local Gauleiters, who presented them in recognition of loyal, outstanding service to the Party by Party members in the Gau during the period of the 'Kampfzeit'. These were recognized Party awards, but were not designated as national awards. In fact, only one Gau badge could be worn at any given time, and none was supposed to be worn when the Golden Party Badge was worn. All of the following Gau badges were worn on the left breast pocket:

1. Sachsen, Bayerische Ostmark, Halle-Merseburg, Hessen-Nassau, Magdeburg-Anhalt, Mecklenburg, Lübeck: This was a common badge for the eight Gaue. It was awarded in silver only. The round 44mm badge was designed in 1933, and consisted of a black enamel swastika with the date '1923' or '1925' in the center, affixed to a silver oakleaf wreath. The reverse bore the manufacturer's logo and, usually, the silver content designation (800).

B. Regnemer

Obverse　　　　　　　　　　Reverse

O. Spronk

Hitler greets Julius Streicher and other Gauleiters at a mass rally in 1937. Most of the Gauleiters shown are wearing the Common Gau badge.

GAU BERLIN COMMEMORATIVE BADGE
(Gau-Traditionsabzeichen Berlin)

The first award of the Gau Berlin Commemorative badge was made by Dr. Joseph Goebbels, Gauleiter of Berlin, on the 29th of October 1936, shortly after the badge was instituted. It came in two classes - silver and gold, with only approximately 30 of the gold ever being awarded. Both classes were identical in design: a 41.5mm round badge with a green enamel oakleaf wreath, with the word 'Berlin' at the bottom, surrounding the early Party national emblem with the date '1926' on the left, and '1936' on the right. The reverse of the badge bore the manufacturer's logo, and serial number.

The badge was worn on the left breast pocket.

Obverse

Reverse

Johannes Engel wearing his Gau Berlin Commemorative Badge.

GAU ESSEN COMMEMORATIVE BADGE
(Gau-Traditionsabzeichen Essen)

Instituted by Gauleiter Josef Terboven in 1935, it served to commemorate the tenth anniversary of the founding of the Gau.   It came in two classes - silver and gold, and was worn on the left breast pocket.   Both classes were identical in appearance: a vertical sword over a crossed hammer and pick.   The head of the hammer bears the date '1925', while the head of the pick has '1935'.   The reverse has the manufacturer's logo - Hoffstätter, Bonn.   The badge measured 53mm high, and 31mm at its widest point.

The design of the badge appears to be an exact copy of a 'golden' 1932 Essen rally badge.

Obverse   **Reverse**

1932 Essen rally badge from which the design of the Gau badge appears to have been taken. (Exact scale)

GAU THÜRINGEN COMMEMORATIVE BADGE
(Traditions-Gauabzeichen für Thüringer)

The Thüringen Gau badge was instituted by Gauleiter Fritz Sauckel in June 1933 as an award for the 1,000 oldest Party members in the Gau. Its design was taken from the Gau Thüringen rally badge of the same date. Little information has appeared in contemporary publications concerning this badge.

It would appear that two classes, rather than one, were awarded - silver and gold. This is borne out by the designation of 'Silber' on the award document that accompanied the honor badge. However, this is nothing more than an educated guess.

The honor badge took the form of a stylized eagle clutching a swastika bearing the inscription "NSDAP für treue Thüring." The usual badge is heavy silver, and bears the award issue number on the reverse.

Pete Malone

Obverse　　　　　　　　**Reverse**

208

The '800' silver content mark was usually stamped on the bottom of the Gau Thüringen Badge.

NOTE:
The case for the Gau Thüringen Badge was in dark red, pebbled leather with no inscription on the lid. The upper interior lid was in medium blue satin and the lower section was in dark blue velvet.

GAU BADEN COMMEMORATIVE BADGE
(Gau-Ehrenzeichen des Gaues Baden)

Instituted in 1933 by Robert Wagner, the Baden Gauleiter, the Gau Baden badge was in two classes - silver and gold. Worn on the left breast pocket, it measured 35mm wide and 46mm high. It took the form of an oval oakleaf wreath with the inscription 'Gau Baden' in black at the bottom. In the center was the early form of the Party eagle.

A round woman's brooch measuring 27mm, and having the same basic design, was also produced.

The reverse bore the manufacturer's logo. Some pieces also had the Party member's number engraved on the reverse.

 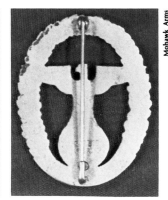

Obverse

Reverse
(The manufacturer is 'F. R. Klett-Karlsruhe')

Hitler and party officials in Weimar, 5 November 1938. Note that the Party leader second from right is wearing the Gau Thüringen Badge.

Brooch version of the Gau Baden badge awarded to female party members authorized to receive it. The badge was awarded only in silver. The round badge measures 27mm. The reverse bears the manufacturer's logo 'Fr. Klett, Karlsruhe'. This specimen bears no Party number on the reverse.

EAST HANOVER GAU COMMEMORATIVE BADGE
(Traditionsabzeichen des Gaues Osthannover der NSDAP)

Three classes of this badge (bronze, silver and gold) were instituted by Gauleiter Otto Telschow in July, 1933. Like the other Gau badges, little information on paper has come to light concerning the criteria for award. It was, however, worn on the left breast pocket. At the top of the oval badge, which measured 40mm wide and 50mm

Obverse   Reverse

high, was the Hanover horse in an oval rope. Below this was the inscription "Im Jahre der Nationalsozial. Erhebung Gautag Osthannover" (In the year of the Nazi accession to power - Party District Day East Hanover). Around the outer edge was an oakleaf wreath. The badge was hollow-backed and bore no visible logo.

The date '1933', referring to the date of institution, was immediately below the Hanover horse.

GAU DANZIG COMMEMORATIVE BADGE
(Gau-Traditionsabzeichen des Gaues Danzig-WestpreuBen)

This silver oval badge measured 32mm wide by 40mm high, and was worn on the left breast pocket. Around the outer edge was an oval oakleaf wreath. In the center was a large swastika with the Danzig shield in its middle. Above the swastika was the word 'Alter' and below 'Kämpfer' - or 'Old Fighter'. The exact date of institution is not known, but it is believed to be May, 1939. It was instituted by Gauleiter Albert Forster.

Obverse

Reverse

R. McCarthy

Gauleiter Forster wearing his Gau Danzig Badge during a speech in August, 1939.

211

Variation Danzig Gau Badge
(Not to scale)

GAU EAST PRUSSIA COMMEMORATIVE BADGE
(Gau-Ehrenzeichen des Gaues OstpreuBen)

Gauleiter Erich Koch instituted the Gau East Prussia Commemorative badge in 1938 to mark the tenth Party assembly in Königsberg. The design was the creation of Mssrs. Birth and Grün. The badge came in one class only - silver - and was worn on the left breast pocket. Oval shaped, it measured 38.5mm wide and 50mm high. Approximately 1,000 awards were authorized. The design incorporated the national emblem over the shield of East Prussia, surrounded by an oakleaf wreath. On the reverse was the manufacturer's logo.

Obverse

The reverse is marked 'Wächter u. Lange mittweida 1. SA'. ➤

GAU SUDETENLAND COMMEMORATIVE BADGE
(Gau-Ehrenzeichen des Gaues Sudetenland der NSDAP)

The first award of the Gau Sudetenland Commemorative badge was made by Gauleiter Konrad Henlein at Christmas 1943, making it the last officially recognized Gau badge to be instituted. The gold oval badge depicted a stylized national emblem surrounded by an oakleaf wreath. At the bottom of the wreath was the date '1938' separated by black/red/black enamel (the colors of Gau Sudetenland). The 1938 date reflects the date of the Gau's foundation. The 45mm wide by 55mm high badge was worn on the left breast and ranked below the Iron Cross 1st Class. The reverse was normally plain; however, some examples were produced with the manufacturer's logo and the silver content designation.

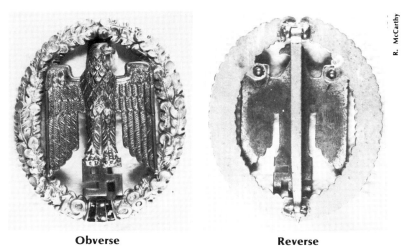

R. McCarthy

Obverse   Reverse

SA-Stabschef Wilhelm Schepmann attends a gathering of high ranking political officials in 1944. He wears the Gau Sudetenland badge below his Iron Cross 1st Class.   213

GAU WARTHE COMMEMORATIVE BADGE
(Gau Wartheland-Traditionsabzeichen)

While the exact date of institution of the Gau Warthe Commemorative badge is not known, it was probably instituted in early 1940 by Gauleiter Arthur Greiser. Two construction techniques were employed in producing the badge - one used a pot-metal base, had four rivets, and the date affixed directly to the bottom of the wreath; while the other used eight rivets, a higher grade base metal, and had the date overlapping the plow. Both were serial numbered, with the first example having the number scratched into the eagle and wreath on the reverse, while the second example had the number engraved at the top of the wreath. Both designs were basically identical, depicting a stylized national emblem with blue enamel swastika over a plow and sword, and finished in a burnished (blackened) color. This was affixed to a gold open-ended wreath measuring 53mm. At the bottom of the wreath was the date '1939' in blue enamel, commemorating the creation of Gau Warthe (26 October 1939) following the dissolution of Poland.

B. Regnemer

Obverse   Reverse

Miniature lapel pin - exact scale.

The badge was worn on the lower left breast.

This is believed to be the only Gau badge which had a miniature. The 23mm miniature was identical in design in every respect to the standard-sized badge.

This Warthe Gau Badge with Brilliants was uncovered by American Occupation Troops in Austria, along with several ornate inlaid rifles. To date, the original owner has not been ascertained.

POTSDAM BADGE
(Potsdam-Abzeichen)

An estimated 100,000 persons attended the first Reich Youth Day rally held in Potsdam on 1/2 October 1932 under the auspices of Reich Youth Leader Baldur von Schirach. A bronze badge served to commemorate the rally of the various youth organizations. The 23mm by 48.5mm badge was worn on the left breast pocket by members of the Hitler Youth (and all its related organizations) and SA who were in attendance. The badge later achieved semi-official national recognition.

Obverse

Reverse

215

The inscription on the badge, 'N S I. Reichsjugendtag 1932' (National Socialist 1st National Youth Day 1932), was simply descriptive of the event.

Manufacturer's variations were produced in silver or with a flat gray finish in addition to the normal bronze.

The reverse of the badge bears the manufacturer's logo.

Miniature lapel pin, exact scale.

LONG SERVICE AWARDS OF THE NSDAP
(Dienstauszeichnungen der NSDAP)

On 2 April 1939, Hitler ordered the institution of long service awards for qualified Party members - both male and female. The first awards were made on 30 January 1940. Service time with the Party was counted from February 1925, with the time from that date to 30 January 1933 counting double in recognition of the 'Kampfzeit' (Time of Struggle) by members of the Old Guard. Accumulated service time had to be unbroken with the following exceptions:

1. Compulsory military duty, providing it did not exceed two years duration.

2. Service against the Bolsheviks during the period 1936 to 1939 (The Spanish Civil War).

3. Military service after September 1939.

Service in any of the Party formations in any rank (Party members serving in Hitler Youth organizations were required to hold officer rank) was counted towards total accumulated service time.

The awards came in three classes as follows:

(a) 3rd Class: A bronze medal, awarded for ten years Party service, normally measuring 43mm, and suspended from a 30mm brown ribbon with two white stripes at each edge. The basic design of all three classes was identical - a national emblem surrounded by an oakleaf wreath in the center of an 'Ordenskreuz' with rays projecting between the arms. The reverse repeated this design; however, instead of the national emblem, the inscription "Treue für Führer und Volk" (Loyalty to Leader and People) was inscribed within the wreath. Two manufacturing techniques were employed to produce this one class - a single stamping that resulted in a finished basic medal, and one of two-part construction having the basic cross joined with the wreath and national emblem on the front. The manufacturer's hallmark was normally stamped into the suspension ring.

Obverse   **Reverse**

(b) 2nd Class: The 15 Year Service medal had the same basic design as the 3rd Class.   This award was in silver, with blue enamel on the arms of the cross and the center of the wreath (both front and back).   It was a thicker three-piece assembly, with the wreath portion front and back added to the cross.   The inscription on the reverse was silver in blue enamel instead of raised lettering as in the case of the 3rd Class.   The suspension ribbon measured 30mm, and was blue with two silver-gray stripes at each edge.

Obverse   **Reverse**

(c) 1st Class: The gold 25 Year Service medal was identical in design to the 2nd Class, except that gold replaces the silver, and white enamel replaces the blue.   The 30mm suspension ribbon was red with two off-white stripes at the edges with a gold stripe running between them.   There were cases where this grade was posthumously   217

Obverse

Reverse

25 Year NSDAP Party Service medal for women recipients. It was worn on the upper breast or lapel as a brooch. Notice the completely different style suspension loop, and the fact that a man's award could not be modified to incorporate this suspension.

Lid of the 10 Year NSDAP Service medal case - brown with a gold national emblem. The lower interior is off-white, flocked, and compartmented.

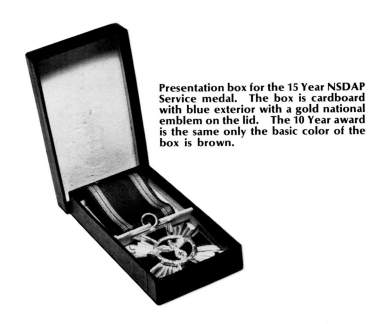

Presentation box for the 15 Year NSDAP Service medal. The box is cardboard with blue exterior with a gold national emblem on the lid. The 10 Year award is the same only the basic color of the box is brown.

Presentation case for the 25 Year NSDAP Service Medal. The exterior is dark red with a gold embossed eagle while the upper lid interior is white satin and the lower interior section is recessed beige velvet.

Gauleiter Albert Hoffmann wearing his ribbon bar with metal devices on the NSDAP Service Ribbons.

awarded to higher ranking Party members who had not accumulated the required time, but had died 'in the line of duty'.

In the case of men, the award was worn on the medal bar above the left breast pocket, and ranked behind the military service awards (except in the case of the SS, who wore the award in front of their military service decorations).   When the ribbon bar was worn, a metal device (a national emblem in a round oakleaf wreath) in bronze, silver, or gold was affixed to the corresponding ribbon.   Women wore the award around their neck or as a brooch medal suspended from a 15mm ribbon.   Female awards were often modified to have an elongated suspension ring to accommodate the suspension bow.   All three classes could be worn at the same time.   221

Award citation for the 10 Year NSDAP Service Medal in bronze, presented to Karl Wolff, 30 January 1941.

Wm. Chizar

Besitzurkunde
Dem Parteigenossen
Karl Frank
verleihe ich hiermit
die Dienstauszeichnung
der NSDAP in Silber
für 15 jährige aktive
Dienstzeit in der NSDAP

München, den 30.1.1940.

NATIONALSOZIALISTISCHE DEUTSCHE ARBEITERPARTEI

Award Citation for the 15 Year NSDAP Service Medal in silver presen to Karl Frank, 30 January 1940.

GERMAN ORDER
(Deutscher Orden)

On February 11, 1942, Adolf Hitler introduced an award which he personally designated as the Party's highest decoration when he awarded a newly created order posthumously to Reichsminister Dr. Fritz Todt, who had been killed in an air accident. From its first appearance on 11 February 1942 to the last recorded date of award on 28 April 1945, the award was to be known by a multitude of designations. Hitler most commonly referred to it as the German Order (Deutscher Orden). Other designations were:

a. Der deutsche Orden für die höchsten Verdienste (The German Order for the highest Merit) - A German newspaper called it this when commenting on the award made to Dr. Todt.

b. Die oberste Stufe des Deutschen Ordens (The highest Class of the German Order) - A German newspaper article called it this when describing an award made by Hitler on 9 June 1942, three days after the death of SS-Obergruppenführer Reinhard Heydrich.

c. Die oberste Stufe des Deutschen Ordens mit Schwertern (The highest Class of the German Order with Swords) - An official description in the citation accompanying the award presented to Gauleiter Josef Bürckel on 3 October 1944.

d. Das Goldene Kreuz des Deutschen Ordens mit Eichenlaub und Schwertern (The Golden Cross of the German Order with Oakleaves and Swords) - This description accompanied the award presented to Reichsarbeitsführer Konstantin Hierl on 24 February 1945.

e. Das Goldene Kreuz des Deutschen Ordens (The Golden Cross of the German Order) - This description was given to the awards presented to Gauleiter Karl Hanke on 12 April 1945 and Reichsjugendführer Artur Axmann on 28 April 1945.

Most of the official designations indicate that there was more than one class of the award; the classes are believed to be as follows:

a. Commander's Cross: Oakleaf wreath and crossed swords suspension worn about the neck from a 45mm ribbon of red with black and white outer edges (this was identical to the ribbon worn on the Blood Order).

b. Second Class: National emblem on suspension loop worn from a neck ribbon as above.

c. Third Class: Pin back version worn on the left breast pocket, and completely plain on the reverse.

It is also possible that the succession of awards was: German Order First Class with Swords, German Order First Class and German Order Second Class. Which of these two successions, if either, is correct is not known, but the fact remains that three distinct grades did exist. Since there is positive proof that the first two recipients were awarded the Order with swords (even before the swords were officially designated), this would indicate that all the known recipients received the swords by virtue of their position and level of service to the Reich. There is no known case where the lesser grades were ever presented. Documented recipients were as follows:

1. Reichsminister für Bewaffnung u. Munition Dr. Fritz Todt - 11 February 1942. (Posthumous)

2. SS-Obergruppenführer Reinhard Heydrich - 9 June 1942. (Posthumous)

3. NSKK-Korpsführer Adolf Hühnlein - 22 June 1942. (Posthumous)

4. SA-Stabschef Viktor Lutze - 8 May 1943. (Posthumous)

5. Gauleiter Josef Bürckel - 3 October 1944. (Committed suicide in November 1944.)

6. Generalmajor Rudolf Schmundt - 7 October 1944. (Posthumous)

7. Reichsarbeitsführer Konstantin Hierl - 24 February 1945.

8. Gauleiter Karl Hanke - 12 April 1945.

9. Gauleiter Karl Holz - 19 April 1945.

10. Reichsjugendführer Artur Axmann - 28 April 1945. Axmann's citation is to be found in the 'Völkischer Beobachter' of April 29, 1945. It is again referred to as 'The Golden Cross of the German Order'. (Axmann was simultaneously awarded the E.K., I Class.) Interestingly, the article refers to Axmann as "the third living German, after Gauleiters Hanke and Holz, to receive this award." It appears that Konstantin Hierl was forgotten. (Gauleiter Holz was killed in the fighting for Nürnberg, and Hanke was executed by the Poles, thus making Hierl and Axmann the only two recipients of the award to survive the war and its consequences.)

11. Grandadmiral Karl Dönitz - May 1945. Grandadmiral Dönitz states that he also was rendered the award, and addressed it as the Chancellery German Order (Kanzlei Deutscher Orden).[6] There is some evidence that Reichsführer-SS Heinrich Himmler also received the award, but the date and circumstances are not known.[7] It is unlikely that there were other awards, but no records exist to confirm or refute this possibility.

Hitler viewed the award as his personal decoration, to be bestowed only upon worthy persons who had rendered great service to him, the Party and the German people. For this reason, and by virtue of the fact that the reverse bears his signature, the Order is often referred to as the 'Hitler Order'. Additionally, since five of the awards were presented posthumously, it was also referred to as the 'Order of the

---

[6] *Personal interview between Grandadmiral Dönitz and author.*

[7] *Reichsführer-SS Himmler was considered for the award in May 1944, but in fact never received it. Speer's memoirs confirm this. Also, it is difficult to imagine the* V.B. *or* Das Schwarze Korps *ignoring such an event if it happened.*

Dead'. Upon its introduction in 1942, the German Order was viewed as the highest award that could be presented by the Party. It is very confusing why it was never given national recognition, since other Party awards had been so designated. Dr. Doehle, the official Chancellery secretary for orders and decorations, makes no mention of the award in his official publications.

The basic cross of the three classes measured 50mm. The Oakleaves and Swords added another 52mm from the top arm of the Cross, while the suspension of the second class of the German Order measured only 30mm. In the center of the cross was the standard pattern Golden Party badge, which measured only 21.5mm in this case. The black enamel cross is bordered by detailed golden oakleaves; between each arm is the national emblem in gilt. The reverse repeats this design except for the center where a facsimile of Hitler's signature is engraved in gold on black enamel. The reverse of the breast badge is plain, and void of any markings. The German Order was produced by the Wilhelm Deumer firm in Ludenscheid, while the suspension ribbon, measuring 45mm wide, was done by Karl Loy of Munich.

Littlejohn/Dodkins

Obverse   Reverse

Standard pattern German Order 1st Class. This is identical in design to that first awarded on 11 February 1942.

Obverse   **Reverse**

B. Hritz

Pin-back version of the German Order. The breast badge is slightly convex. The reverse is void of any design or markings, and is highly polished.

Pin-back version of the German Order in original presentation case. The case is red without lid designation. The interior of the upper lid is white satin, while the lower compartmented section is red velvet.

An unexplainable variation of the German Order,   produced by the Deumer firm in Ludenscheid, incorporated the same style Oakleaves and Swords found on the Knight's Cross to the Iron Cross, except that here they are finished in gold.   The reverse of the sword hilts are finished as well.   Yet another variation is shown here which has an identical standard pattern suspension loop, but which features the swords passing through the arms of the cross.

According to Albert Speer, the basic design for the German Order was executed by Benno von Arendt, in response to a personal commission by Hitler.

Obverse   Reverse

Design anomaly of the German Order 1st Class with swords. Note that the national emblems between the arms of the cross are smaller, and unfinished on the reverse. Note also that the suspension loop is identical in both patterns.

Variation German Order 1st Class with original presentation case. The case is dark red and void of any distinctive markings. The interior of the lid is white satin, while the lower section is burgundy velvet. The lower section is compartmented to house the cross and the suspension loop.

The only description of the award document is provided by the widow of Konstantin Hierl, the 7th recipient of the German Order.[8] The parchment document measured 420mm high by 340mm wide, with the text finished in gold. The document is contained in a leather casette, 40mm thick, with a gold national emblem on the front.

The actual award was encased in a hard presentation case. At least three different versions of the case are known to exist.

---

[8] *Information provided by the noted German research historian, Dr. K.-G. Klietmann.*

Funeral pillow displaying some of the awards bestowed upon Dr. Fritz Todt. The two most significant awards are the German Order (awarded posthumously by Hitler), and the National Prize for Art and Science.

Jim Jones

The award document above was presented to Konstantin Hierl on 24 February 1945 along with his Golden Cross of the German Order with Oakleaves and Swords. The Document is fired gold on parchment and the white leather cover is bordered in gold with a metal gold eagle.

National Sport Awards

231

GERMAN NATIONAL SPORT BADGE
(Deutsches Reichssportabzeichen)

The 1913 Olympic Games generated considerable interest in physical training within Germany, which resulted in the institution of a national gymnastics and sports badge by the German National Committee for Physical Training. Initially, the badge was in bronze and gold, and only men were eligible to receive it. However, a silver version was introduced in 1920, and in 1921 women became eligible for the award. After 1921, criteria for the award were as follows:

a. Bronze: Awarded to men and women between the ages of 18 and 32 who passed five parts of the national test within a twelve month period. Within each of the five tests were sub-tests that were based on physical skill, endurance and time. Levels for qualification were less for women than men. One exercise from each group was selected, and had to be performed under supervision.

b. Silver: Awarded to men and women between the ages of 18 and 32 who passed the tests for a total of eight years, or to persons between 32 and 40 who passed the tests during a twelve month period.

c. Gold: Awarded to men and women between the ages of 18 and 32 who passed the tests for a total of seven consecutive years once the silver badge had been awarded. Persons over 40 years of age need only pass the tests during a single twelve month period.

The cloth version was in silver-gray thread on black.

A professional policeman all of his adult life, Hauptkommissar Alois Tress entered police service with the Gendarmerie in 1924. When the war broke out, he was on active duty; advancing from the rank of NCO to Hauptmann in the Army Field Police. The men under his command carried on an active campaign against partisans for which he was awarded, among other decorations, the Eastern People's Decoration for Bravery First Class. As a policeman and military officer, he was required to maintain his athletic proficiency. He wears the SA Military Sports Badge in bronze on the left, and the German National Badge for Physical Training in bronze on the right. The specimen shown is the pattern with the 'DRA' monogram and is also void of the swastika, indicating award prior to 1937.

The oval badge measuring 48mm high by 39mm wide, bore the initials 'DRA' (Deutscher Reichs-Ausschuss) intertwined with, and surrounded by, an oakleaf wreath with a bow ribbon at the bottom. The reverse bore the manufacturer's logo. The badge was worn on the left breast pocket of any uniform. A miniature version was authorized for wear on the left lapel, and a cloth version was authorized for wear on the athletic shirt. This pattern badge remained in existence until 1933.

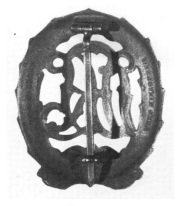

Obverse   **Reverse**

In 1933 the control of sports was placed under the Deutscher Reichsbund für Leibesübungen (DRL - German National Physical Training Union). The same basic badge was retained except that the 'DRA' was replaced by 'DRL'. Three classes were awarded, and criteria for award remained the same.

On 1 September 1937, this badge was again modified to incorporate the swastika, which was superimposed over the bow at the bottom of the wreath. In 1938 alone the following awards were presented:

a. Bronze: 86,624

b. Silver: 8,072

c. Gold: 1,935

By the end of 1938, a total of 766,025 bronze awards had been presented to men and women.

Third Place bronze oakleaf awarded for running the 1500 meter run during the Nordmark Light Athletic Team Championships in 1939.

On 18 November 1942 a 4th Class award was added to be presented to members of the armed forces who "in spite of considerable disability, manage to attain the average level of proficiency in the performance of the test-exercises for those types of disability." The badge was identical in design to the 1937 pattern DRL badge, except that the initials were in silver and the wreath was in gold.

The first award was rendered in December 1942, by the Reichsportführer, Hans von Tschammer und Osten. By March 1945, approximately 10,000 of this grade had been awarded.

DRL INDIVIDUAL COMPETITION AWARD

Individual incentive awards were instituted by the German National Physical Training Union (DRL) to be presented to the first, second and third place competitors in an athletic competition. While various awards were used to achieve this purpose, ranging from medals to medallions, the most commonly used award was the oakleaf - the German symbol for strength.

A single oakleaf in bronze (third place), silver (second place) or gold (first place) was awarded for corresponding placement in a competition. Attached to the oakleaf was an orange and white cord bearing the symbol of the DRL. This in turn was affixed to an award certificate by means of a single prong. The certificate bore the name of the recipient, the athletic club that he represented, the event, and the qualifying time, distance, etc.

The award was not intended to be worn, but served more as a remembrance of the event. This particular award did not receive recognition outside the DRL.

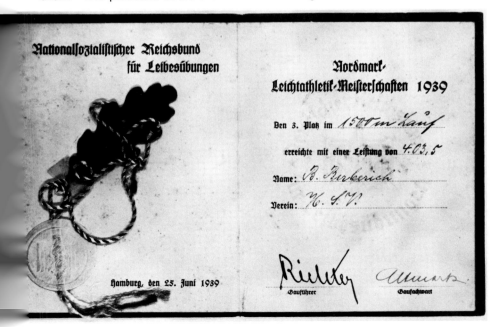

Deutsches Reichs-Sportabzeichen

Ersatz-Urkunde für Wiederholung der Prüfungen

Nur zugleich mit dem ausgefüllten und vollzogenen Urkundenheft und den vorausgegangenen bereits bestätigten Wiederholungsurkunden vorzulegen

Das Abzeichen wurde unter Nr. 303919 am 7. November 1934 erstmalig erworben

Vor- und Zuname des Bewerbers:

Horst Collier

Geboren am 23 Juli 1916

Wohnort (Ort): Berlin

(Straße, Hausnummer) Türkenstraße 9?

Vereinsangehörigkeit des Bewerbers: Brandenburg

Name des Verbandes: Deutscher Leichtathletik Verb

Bewerbung um das Sportabzeichen in: ~~Gold~~ Silber

(Nichtzutreffendes ist zu streichen)

Zu beziehen durch die

Geschäftsstelle des Deutschen Reichsbundes für Leibesübungen

Berlin-Charlottenburg 2, Hardenbergstraße 42-43. Fernruf: C 1 Steinplatz 8171

Der Bewerber hat die Prüfungen der GRUPPE 3 erfüllt, indem er

(Von einem der Sportzeugen eigenhändig mit Tinte auszufüllen)

Eigenhändige Unterschrift des Bewerbers

(Vor- und Zuname)

Ort:

Datum: 5 September 19 35

Eigenhändige Unterschrift der beiden bei der Abnahme zugegen gewesenen Sportzeugen:

(Vor- und Zuname)

1. 2.

Vereinsangehörigkeit   Vereinsangehörigkeit

Der Bewerber hat die Prüfungen der GRUPPE 4 erfüllt, indem er

(Von einem der Sportzeugen eigenhändig mit Tinte auszufüllen)

Eigenhändige Unterschrift des Bewerbers

(Vor- und Zuname)

Stempel des die Prüfung abnehmenden Verbandes (Gau oder Kreis)

Ort:

Datum: 19

Eigenhändige Unterschrift der beiden bei der Abnahme zugegen gewesenen Sportzeugen

(Vor- und Zuname)

1. 2.

Vereinsangehörigkeit   Vereinsangehörigkeit

The award certificate and qualification test record are combined in this particular example. The cover page to the left indicates that the first year's award (serial number 303919) was presented on 7 November 1934. Tests for the second year award were completed on 5 September 1935 (see page 2 at right), 13 September, and on 19 August 1935, resulting in the award of the National Sports badge in silver.

NATIONAL YOUTH SPORTS BADGE
(Reichsjugendsportabzeichen)

In 1925, the DRA established the National Youth Sports badge, which was to be awarded to school-aged children. From 1925 to 1927, the award was restricted to males only, but in 1928 it was extended to females. From 1925 to 1938 a total of 273,992 awards was rendered to males and females meeting the necessary qualifications.[1]

The award was given only in silver, and was restricted to children under 18 years of age.

In 1937 the swastika was added to the award, giving it its final form. The award took the form of a 15mm round stickpin which was worn on the left lapel. The initials 'RJA' (Reichs-Jugend-Abzeichen) were surrounded by an oakleaf wreath with a swastika at the bottom. A cloth version measuring 45mm was worn on the athletic shirt.

Awards of this badge ceased by order of the Reichssportführer on 1 July 1942.

---

[1] *Der Schulungsbrief*, No. 2, 1939, Berlin 1939.

The cloth version was in silver-gray thread on black.

The reverse of the stickpin bore the manufacturer's logo.

SA-SPORT BADGE
(SA-Sportabzeichen)

The SA-Sport badge was instituted by SA-Stabschef Ernst Röhm on 28 November 1933, and could only be awarded to SA and SS members. It took the form of a 57mm Roman broad sword pointing upwards, superimposed over a swastika, which was encircled by an oakleaf wreath. All subsequent badges retained the same design, with only the inscription on the reverse changing, thus allowing an award to be properly dated. The 1934-1935 pattern bore the inscription 'Eigentum des Chefs des Ausbildungswesens' (Property of the Head of Physical Conditioning). This period badge was in bronze only.

Hitler quickly saw the benefits of using such an award to stimulate the overall physical development of young German men. On 15 February 1935 he decreed that the SA-Sport badge be given official status, and expanded it to include a silver and gold class. Most importantly, he opened it to the German public at large. Initially, the distinction between the bronze, silver and gold awards was a degree of proficiency. However, after April, 1936, a point system was established as criteria for award. An entry indicating which level award was earned was made in the individual's Ausweis (the personal record each individual carried).

On 18 March 1937 the award was further upgraded by requiring that each recipient pass proficiency tests annually to be able to retain the award. Failure to do so meant that the award had to be surrendered to the SA-Sport-Hauptstelle. The badges during the period 1935-1939 bore the inscription 'Eigentum der SA-Sportabzeichen-Hauptstelle' (Property of the SA Sport Badge Head Department) on the reverse.

Possibly as a fore-warning of things to come, Hitler changed the official designation on 19 January 1939 from 'SA-Sportabzeichen' to 'SA-Wehrabzeichen' (SA Military Defense Badge). He personally challenged every able-bodied German male to try to earn the award, which now took on a greater significance in that it resulted in the training of potential combatants in military related areas. Hitler Youth members who had reached the age of 16 and all other German boys who had reached the age of 17 were 'encouraged' to compete for the award. Furthermore, military veterans who were physically able were required to join 'Wehrmannschaften', or military defense teams, to retain their physical and mental abilities. The reverse of the badge for the period 1939-1944 bore the inscription 'Eigentum der Obersten SA.-Führung' (Property of the SA Supreme Command), indicating that it could be recalled at any time for whatever reason.[2] A booklet specifically devoted to recording the tests required was issued, and upon successful completion, an official award document contained in it was approved and signed.

Metal, officially-awarded version.

Reverse of the 1939-1944 Pattern SA Sport badge.

---

[2]*A specimen has been encountered bearing only the RZM logo on the reverse.*

Cloth version for the athletic uniform. The badge is in the corresponding grade (bronze: bronze; silver: gray-white; gold: yellow) on either white or black background.

This elderly SA defender of Metz, September 1944, wears the SA-Sport Badge on his left breast pocket.

Testing for the award was broken down into three main groups (physical fitness, military defense and field exercises), which were in turn broken down into subdivisions. Probably the most trying test was the long distance road march with heavy pack. Upon successful completion of the tests, awards were rendered on the basis of accumulated points and age as follows:

a. Bronze: Men under the age of 35 who successfully passed the test requirements during a twelve month period received a solid bronze badge.

b. Silver: Men under the age of 35 who successfully passed the test for five consecutive years, or men between the ages of 35 and 40 who passed the tests during a twelve month period received a silver-colored badge.

c. Gold: Men who had been awarded the silver badge, and continued to pass the tests annually for an additional six years, or men over 40 who passed the tests during a twelve month period received the badge finished in a gold color.

A variation exists for which there is not yet an explanation. The badge is identical to the standard design, except that the finish is different. The sword and swastika are silver-colored, while the wreath is gold. This silver-gold combination may have been a forerunner of the SA Military Sports Badge for War Wounded, which was adopted in 1943, but with a different design. The National Sports badge, adopted in 1942, incorporated this silver-gold combination, and remained unchanged in design. Possibly this particular pattern SA Sport badge was intended as an interim award for war wounded.

Badges earned prior to the outbreak of the war bore the serial number of the award on the reverse of the badge; however, this practice was discontinued after 1939. The badge bearing the number 1,000,000 was awarded on 10 December 1936. By the end of 1943, more than 2.5 million badges had been awarded.

The badge was worn on the left breast pocket, and was authorized for wear on military and political uniforms. When in civilian clothes, a miniature badge in the form of a stickpin was worn on the left lapel. Authorized recipients were permitted to purchase a duplicate badge, but these were not marked with the serial number. A cloth version of the badge was authorized for wear on the athletic uniform.

The badge measured 57mm high and 44mm wide.

Special presentation case for the SA Sport badge. This particular case is completely different from the standard plain off-white cardboard box normally used. The case is brown wood with the early pattern SA national emblem on the lid, backed by a thin, light-colored wood. The interior of the case is red velvet. The area of the clasp is recessed.

Der Inhaber dieſer URKUNDE hat die

LEISTUNGSPRÜFUNG

mit _813_ Punkten beſtanden.

Ihm wurde am _11. 5._ 19 _38_ das

SA-Sportabzeichen

in

BRONZE

Beſ.-Zeugn. Nr. _001369799_ verliehen.

Ort _Hamburg-Altona_

den _2 4. Feb. 19 39_

Unterſchrift
Oberſturmbannführer

SA Sport badge award certificate in bronze.   These certificates were included in the SA-Sportabzeichen Übungsbuch where the records of qualification and accumulated points were recorded.   This award was presented to Heinz Eylmann, a member of SA-Standarte 31 of Hamburg-Altona.   The award number on the certificate was the same number that would be stamped on the reverse of the badge.   Notice that the test was completed in May 1938, but the award was not approved until February 1939.

Bob McCarthy

Variation of the SA Sport Badge depicting an anchor stamped into the central motif. Details for such a variation are lacking, but it is possible that it was intended for possible award to the Marine units of the SA and NSKK.

SA MILITARY SPORTS BADGE FOR WAR WOUNDED
(SA-Wehrabzeichen für Kriesgversehrte)

On 8 October 1943 the Stabschef of the SA ordered that an additional set of criteria for the earning of the SA Military Defense badge (SA-Wehrabzeichen) be established, and a corresponding badge be instituted. This was done to allow military wounded to compete for a specially designed badge so they might in turn retain their military and mental skills. The badge was basically identical to the standard pattern SA-Wehrabzeichen, but measured 60mm high and 47mm wide, with a 'Wolfsangel-Rune' superimposed over the hilt of the sword at the base of an elongated oakleaf wreath. The swastika and the general pattern of the badge were more stylized than the basic pattern. The reverse did not have the serial number of the award recorded, in keeping with wartime practice. It did, however, bear the RZM manufacturer's logo.

On 15 December 1943 the specific criteria were announced. The award could be earned by any male person over the age of 18 who was wounded or disabled in, or as a result of, the war. That person had to meet a set of standards commensurate to his disability, which was established on an individual basis by a competent medical authority.

The first award of this decoration was made by SA Stabschef Schepmann on 12 July 1944 when he presented 100 badges to wounded military veterans. The badge was worn on the left breast pocket.

It is probable that the badge was awarded in bronze, silver and gold versions. The piece shown is silver. Since the base metal was zinc, the badge was apt to lose its color and revert to a dull gray finish.

It appears that the badge was only produced by Deschler and Son of Munich.   243

Obverse   **Reverse**
Example piece shown is silver over zinc.

ACHIEVEMENT AND CHAMPIONSHIP BADGES OF THE NSRL & DRL
(Leistungs-und Meisterschaftsabzeichen des Deutschen Reichsbundes für Leibesübungen)

The first award created by the National Socialist Physical Training League (Nationalsozialistischer Reichsbund für Leibesübungen NSRL) was the Championship badge (Meisterschaftsabzeichen), which was introduced on 14 November 1935. In February 1937, two additional badges were created by the National Sports Leader to recognize achievement in the sports field. In 1938 the NSRL became the German National League for Physical Training (Deutscher Reichsbund für Leibesübungen - DRL), but the earlier awards were retained without modification or change in purpose.

The awards were as follows:

a. Bronze with date: Worn for one year only; it was given in recognition of excellence in a single sport.

b. Bronze without date: Permanent award given for excellence in multiple sports.

c. Silver with date: Worn for one year only; it was given as a prize to the runner-up in a single German national championship athletic event.

d. Silver without date: Permanent award given for excellence in representing Germany in international competitions.

e. Gold: Awarded to the national champion in each sports event. Even though the badge was dated, it could be worn permanently. This badge was first awarded in 1935.

The bronze, silver and gold awards were in stickpin form, and were worn on the left lapel.   A cloth version was introduced as well for the bronze and silver awards, and was worn on the athletic uniform.

The reverse of the stickpins were plain.

Award in bronze.   Example shown is with the date of competition.

Silver award.   Example shown is with the date of competition.   The gold award for National Champions is identical in design, but finished in gold.

Example of the award worn on the athletic uniform...bronze on black (to exact scale).

245

HEAVY ATHLETICS BADGE
(Schwerathleten-Abzeichen)

A badge to recognize proficiency in heavy athletics was instituted in 1937. The only examples observed thus far have been in bronze, but it is possible that such a badge also existed in silver and gold. Heavy athletics involved the more muscular activities such as boxing, weight lifting, wrestling and similar sports.

The obverse of the badge depicts the NSRL/DRL organizational eagle superimposed over a set of weights. It is encircled by an oval oakleaf wreath with a bow and shield at the bottom depicting the sport (wrestling, boxing, weight lifting, etc.) The reverse has a horizontal pin, and bears the manufacturer's logo at the bottom.

The badge measures 38mm high by 42mm wide.

Obverse   **Reverse**

GERMAN MOTOR SPORT BADGE
(Deutsches Motorsportabzeichen)

Adolf Hitler instituted the German Motor Sport badge (Deutsches Motorsportabzeichen) on 18 February 1938. It was to be awarded to German men who had successfully engaged in national and international driving competitions. The initial criteria were rather vague, indicating that award was to be given to those who broke speed records, won endurance competitions, etc. However, on 1 November 1938 NSKK-Korpsführer Hühnlein established a more defined criteria for award based on a point system. Points could be amassed during the course of a competition year, with awards as follows:

    a.   badge in iron - 3rd Class - 50 points

    b.   badge in silver - 2nd Class - 100 points

    c.   badge in gold - 1st Class - 150 points

Points could be accumulated based on the finish in a competition. For example, winning first prize in an international competition would earn the winner a total of 12 points, while a national competition win would earn only 8 points.

NSKK-Korpsführer Hühnlein awards the German Motor Sports badge for the first time on 18 February 1939 in Berlin. Presentation of the 1st Class award in gold was made to Staffelführer Caracciola.

The first presentation of the awards was made on 18 February 1939, the anniversary of the institution of the award. On this date awards were presented for the competition year 1938, with the following number of awards being presented:

a. 1st Class in gold - 2. Recipients: Bernd Rosemeyer and Rudolf Caracciola

b. 2nd Class in silver - 4

c. 3rd Class in iron - 23

Awards were made annually. At the awards ceremony on 20 April 1941 for the competition year 1940, there were no gold and only one silver award presented. The total number of awards bestowed from the date of institution is believed to be as follows:

a. 1st Class in gold: 91

b. 2nd Class in silver: 93

c. 3rd Class in iron: 314

The badge was presented in a black case, and was worn on the lower left breast. No award document accompanied the presentation.

The badge was designed by Paul Casberg, and took the form of a flying eagle clutching a wheel superimposed on a swastika encircled by an oakleaf wreath. The reverse of the badge bore the manufacturer's logo, a patent designation for the design, and the silver content designation - normally '800'. The circular badge measured 48mm.

| Obverse | Reverse |

GERMAN AIRSPORT LEAGUE BALLOONIST BADGE
(Deutscher Luftsport Verband (DLV) Ballonabzeichen)

Formed in 1933 to further air-related sports, the Nazi-controlled German Airsport League (Deutscher Luftsport Verband or DLV) was the forerunner of the NSFK, which was formed in 1937.

The DLV was authorized to award qualification badges to persons passing the proficiency tests for Pilot, Radio Operator, and Balloon Pilot.

Two versions of the Balloon Pilot badge existed, with the first pattern being a hot-air balloon surrounded by oakleaves constructed in silver thread on an oval blue-gray

1st Pattern DLV Balloonist Badge

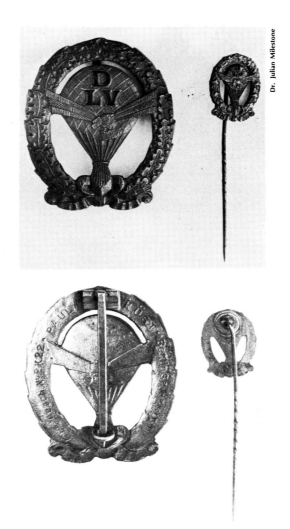

2nd Pattern Balloonist Badge with miniature stickpin

wool.   The first pattern award was worn on the lower left sleeve of the tunic or great-coat.

The second pattern changed drastically.   The bronze oval badge measured 48mm high and 40mm wide.   The design incorporated the hot-air balloon fully surrounded by an oakleaf wreath.   On the face of the balloon was an eagle with outstretched wings over which were the letters 'DLV' in black enamel.   The badge was worn on the left breast pocket of the tunic.   A miniature version was authorized for wear with civilian clothes.

The NSFK Hot-Air Balloon 'Marek-Emmer'.

BADGE FOR FREE BALLOON PILOTS
(Abzeichen für Freiballonführer)

Almost a year after the Air Sport League (Deutsche Luftsport Verband - DLV) had changed into the National Socialist Flying Corps or NSFK, the head of the NSFK, Friedrich Christiansen, established a series of civil air-related badges that were to become badges of distinction for members of the NSFK.   The first such qualification badge was instituted on 10 March 1938, and was awarded to licensed hot-air balloon pilots.   It initially took the form of an oval silver bullion decoration on blue-gray

1st design pattern, 1938

cloth which was sewn to the left breast pocket. The award incorporates the DLV Type 'A' Pilot's badge (black swastika in a circle with outstretched wings) which was superimposed on a hot air balloon encircled by an oakleaf wreath.

In 1939 a second design pattern was introduced: The DLV pattern pilot's badge was removed, thus divesting the badge of any connection with the DLV. The hot-air balloon was retained, and the NSFK emblem was added at the top of the oakleaf wreath. The badge was constructed of metal and had a vertical pin. It was worn on the left breast pocket, and measured 58mm high and 45mm wide. On the reverse was a set of numbers '231240', which probably signified the design patent number.

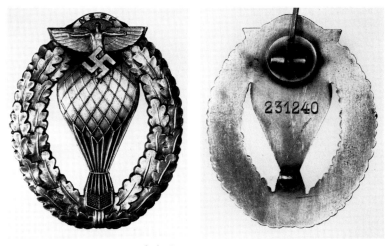

2nd design pattern, 1939

BADGE FOR POWERED AIRCRAFT PILOT
(Abzeichen für Motorflugzeugführer)

Pilots of light powered aircraft who belonged to the National Socialist Flying Corps (Nationalsozialistisches Fliegerkorps - NSFK) were authorized to wear the NSFK Pilot's badge for powered aircraft upon qualification as a civilian pilot. Prior to 1938 a civilian pilot in the NSFK had received only his license. However, on 12 July 1938 NSFK-Korpsführer General der Flieger Christiansen instituted a badge to be awarded to NSFK and NSFK-trained pilots. It took the form of an oval dull-silver bullion design on blue-gray backing. The center motif was a two-seat low-winged monoplane encircled by a wreath. The left portion of the wreath was made up of oakleaves, while the right was composed of laurel leaves. At the base of the wreath was a large silver bullion swastika. This qualification insignia was sewn to the left breast pocket, and was authorized for wear with the NSFK uniform.

1st design pattern

On 1 May 1939 the qualification badge underwent a drastic change in design: most significantly, it was now produced in metal. The change probably came about for two reasons - first, the NSFK emblem had to be incorporated into the design, and, second, a degree of standardization among the sport/qualification badges (e.g., metal) had to be maintained. This second design pattern retained the monoplane (including the swastika on the tail section), but in other respects was quite different. The wreath was composed of oakleaves with the NSFK emblem at the bottom rather than the large swastika. This badge was still worn on the left breast pocket.

2nd design pattern
The clasp ran horizontally rather than vertically. The design patent number '22639' was stamped into the wing on the reverse. The badge measured 57mm high, and 48mm wide.

In 1942 the badge again underwent a change in design. The monoplane was replaced by a soaring eagle, and the NSFK emblem was shifted from the bottom of the oakleaf wreath to the top. The badge measured 57mm high and 53mm wide. Instead of the old silver finish of the second design pattern, the third design pattern was a dull gray alloy metal. The badge was worn on the left breast pocket of the NSFK uniform.

3rd design pattern
The clasp was shifted into the vertical position, and the design patent number (in this case 'GM No. 111241') was retained on the reverse.

CIVIL GLIDING PROFICIENCY BADGE
(Segelflieger-Abzeichen)

The daring German pilots of WWI stirred the imagination of the German people, and stimulated a lively interest in flying. However, the Versailles Treaty forbade a German Air Force, which left the only alternative of civilian (commercial or private) flying. Considering the cost of motor-driven aircraft, Germans turned to the less expensive, but equally daring, sport of gliding or soaring. This sport also proved to be an excellent cover for training future pilots for the clandestine Luftwaffe.

Fledgling pilots had to be tested, and were judged, under the rules of the International Aeronautical Federation. Successful completion of the tests earned the pilot a badge, a certificate of proficiency and possibly a qualified pilot's license. The qualification tests and resultant badges were as follows:

a. 'A' Certificate: 30 second free flight with no maneuvers required. This resulted in a badge with one gull inside a solid circle.

b. 'B' Certificate: 60 second free flight with 'S' turn maneuver. This qualification earned the German Glider Permit and a badge with two gulls inside a solid circle.

Oberfeldwebel Otto Gaiser, holder of the Knight's Cross, wears the 'C' Certificate Civil Gliding Proficiency badge on his left breast. This badge ranked below all other military badges.

c. 'C' Certificate: This appears to have been a dual test. One test was administered purely to qualify, while a more rigorous flight test and oral examination was administered to earn the Official Soaring License. It should be noted at this point that there seems to have been a distinction made between gliding and soaring. A badge with three gulls inside a solid circle was awarded in this category.

d. Achievement 'C' Certificate: This is assumed to have been awarded for a long-duration flight exceeding five hours. A badge with three gulls inside an oakleaf wreath running completely around the gulls was awarded for this. The badge was referred to as the 'Leistungsprüfung C' as well as the 'Leistungsabzeichen'.

The cloth badge measured approximately 50mm, and was finished either in silver-gray thread or silver bullion on a blue-gray backing. A smaller badge of white and blue enamel could be worn with civilian clothing. Qualified pilots were authorized to wear the badge when in uniform.

In January 1942 the Leistungsabzeichen was replaced by the newly introduced 'Grosses Segelfliegerabzeichen'. The A, B and lesser form of the C Certificate badges were retained, and continue in use today.

'A' Certificate Badge. Segelflieger-A-Abzeichen Gleitfliegerprüfung 'A'

'B' Certificate Badge. Segelflieger-B-Abzeichen Gleitfleigerprüfung 'B'.

'C' Certificate Badge. Segelflieger-C-Abzeichen Segelfliegerprüfung 'C'.

'C' Certificate badge in metal worn on the lapel of the civilian dress. The gulls are white enamel, the background is blue enamel, and the outer edge is silver. This badge was presented to the author by its recipient, Knight's Cross winner Wilhelm Joswig. The reverse of some badges bear a manufacturer's logo, a serial number, or both.

LARGE GLIDER PILOT'S BADGE
(Grosses Segelfliegerabzeichen)

The NSFK-Korpsführer, General der Flieger Christiansen, instituted the Large Glider Pilot's badge (Grosses Segelfliegerabzeichen) on 26 January 1942. The purpose of the award was to distinguish advanced qualification beyond the already existing NSFK advanced achievement award for gliding, and to provide a counterpart to the gold and silver international gliding awards of the Federation Aeronautique Internationale.

The round dark-silver badge measured 45mm, and showed an oakleaf wreath with the NSFK insigne at the bottom. Attached to this by means of either two rivets or silver solder, were three white sea gulls, representing free flight. The standard issue badge was the property of the NSFK and was serial-numbered. Private purchase badges were not serial-numbered.

Obverse

**Reverse
(Variant pattern)**

Mohawk Arms

**Reverse
(Standard pattern)**

Two award groups were established, and persons in the Luftwaffe and Hitler Youth as well as NSFK members, were eligible to qualify. The criteria for award were as follows:

Group I: (More honorary than earned by test)

a. Recognized achievement in the advancement of military flight proficiency through gliding.

b. Glider pilot achievement

c. Achievement in hand work (probably glider construction)

Group II:

a. Must have been awarded the 2nd Class Glider Pilot's Certificate and successfully achieved an endurance flight of five hours returning to point of origin, or

b. Must have reached an altitude of 3,300 feet three times during the course of a single flight.

Note the Luftwaffe NCO in foreground wearing the Glider Pilot's Badge.

Tentative evidence would indicate that approximately 1,600 awards were rendered from the time of institution to mid-June of the following year. The total number of awards is not known.

While reference is made only to a single design pattern, it is possible that badges were produced with one and two gulls to correspond to the lesser degrees of proficiency found in the NSFK Glider Pilot's badge. This, however, cannot be substantiated.

The badge was presented with an award document, and was worn on the lower left breast of all uniforms.

VERLEIHUNGSURKUNDE NR. 1611

DAS GROSSE DEUTSCHE SEGELFLIEGERABZEICHEN

verleihe ich

NSFK-Obertruppführer

Helmut B e n d e r

auf Grund seiner segelfliegerischen Leistungen
nach Bedingungsgruppe.

Berlin, am 16. Juni 1943.

DER KORPSFÜHRER DES
NS-FLIEGERKORPS

GENERAL DER FLIEGER

Award document (actual size) presented by General der Flieger Christiansen.

Presentation case for the Large Glider Pilot's Badge. (Not to scale)   The title is in gold on a black simulated leather.   Interior of the case is white.

1933 SA-SS SKI COMPETITION BADGE

As part of the national sports program, annual ski competitions were held which pitted various Nazi organizations against one another.   A badge (which varied with each year's competition) was awarded to the winning individuals and teams.   The competition for 1933 was held in the vicinity of Bad Tölz.   The winner's badge took the form of an oval bearing the runic emblems of the SA and SS superimposed on two parallel skis bearing the inscription 'Gau-Schi Meisterschaft' (top ski) 'Oberbayern Tölz 1933' (bottom ski).   The silver award measured 57mm long.   It was worn on the left breast pocket of the uniform and was affixed by a horizontal pin.   The reverse bore the manufacturer's logo.

This Motor-SA Sturmführer wears his 1933 ski championship badge a year after his team won the competition.

SS-Standartenführer Hermann Fegelein

National
Equestrian Awards

GERMAN HORSEMAN'S BADGE
(Deutsches Reiterabzeichen)

In an effort to stimulate interest in horsemanship, the German National Federation for the Breeding and Testing of Thoroughbreds instituted the German Horseman's Badge (Deutsches Reiterabzeichen) on 9 April 1930.   The badge took the design of a mounted horseman surrounded by an oakleaf wreath.   However, at a later date, a Roman letter "R" in a circle was added to the base of the wreath.   The badge, designed by W. Heitinger of Berlin, measured 42mm wide and 52mm high.   Sometime after 1933, the badge received official recognition as a national award.

The badge came in three classes:

a.   3rd Class in bronze: Awarded for success in horse racing.   A total of 61,710 badges was awarded between 1931 and 1942.   (Dates inclusive).

b.   2nd Class in silver: Awarded for success at tournaments and shows.   A total of 6,183 was awarded between 1931 and 1942.   This class was sometimes produced from genuine silver.   These specimens bear the silver content designation "990" stamped at the bottom on the reverse.

c.   1st Class in gold: Awarded for outstanding achievement in equestrian sports.   The 1st Class is rather rare as only 210 badges were awarded between 1931 and 1942.

Obverse   **Reverse**

Herman Fegelein, a recognized equestrian who represented Germany in the Olympics, wears the German Horseman's Badge on his riding habit.

The badge was awarded in a presentation box with a miniature; an award document accompanied it. Approval authority was vested in the Minister of the Interior. It was worn on the lower left breast of any uniform. However, wear on the military uniform was prohibited from 1930 to January 1936.

his badge is found with both a wide well as a needle type pin. The anufacturer's logo was stamped out the outer wreath.

Award Document for the Horseman's Badge in Bronze.

GERMAN (HORSE) DRIVER'S BADGE
(Deutsches Fahrer-Abzeichen)

Shortly after the institution of the German Horseman's Badge, the German National Federation for the Breeding and Testing of Thoroughbreds introduced the German Horse Driver's Badge (Deutsches Fahrer-Abzeichen) on 16 May 1930. This, too, was designed by W. Heitinger, and measured 51.5mm high by 41mm wide. The obverse of the badge depicted a man driving a chariot pulled by two horses, which was surrounded by an oakleaf wreath with a Roman letter "R" in a circle at the base. It is possible that the first design did not incorporate the "R", which was probably introduced at a later date. It would be more appropriate to call the badge the "German Horsedrawn Vehicle Operator's Proficiency Badge."

| Obverse | Reverse |

The badge was awarded in three classes:

a. 3rd Class in bronze: Awarded for success in trotting competitions. A total of 17,376 awards of this class was presented between 1931 and 1942 (dates inclusive).

b. 2nd Class in silver: Awarded for other types of tournament competition. A total of 1,940 was presented between 1931 and 1942.

c. 1st Class in gold: Awarded for outstanding achievement in equestrian sports. A total of 63 1st Class awards was rendered between 1931 and the end of 1939, making this a very rare badge, indeed.

It was necessary for a recipient to have received a lower award before he could be awarded any higher awards, which accounts for the degree of rarity of the higher classes.

The approving authority was the Minister of the Interior. The badge was awarded with an award document, and was worn on the lower left breast.

GERMAN YOUNG HORSEMAN'S BADGE
(Deutsches Jugend-Reiterabzeichen)

Two years later, in July 1932, the Federation instituted the German Young Horseman's Badge (Deutsches Jugend-Reiterabzeichen). This was a 32mm bronze badge, designed by W. Heitinger, which was to be awarded to boys under the age of 17 who had demonstrated a proficiency in horsemanship. From 1932 to the end of the war, a total of 11,097 awards was made. The design was similar to the German Horseman's Badge, but it was round rather than oval.

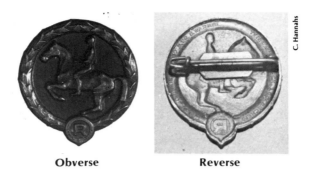

| Obverse | Reverse |

The badge was worn on the left breast pocket, and was accompanied by an award document upon presentation.

GERMAN EXPERT HORSEMAN'S BADGE
(Deutsches Reiterführer-Abzeichen)

There is a degree of confusion surrounding the German Expert Horseman's Badge (Deutsches Reiterführer-Abzeichen) since (1) published regulations give the date of institution as both 23 and 24 February 1937, and (2) regulations as of 1943 state that the badge was in one grade only - silver, while the example illustrated here is bronze.

Obverse of the German Expert Horseman's Badge in bronze.

Reverse of the bronze badge. For those persons who might tend to disqualify this badge because of the needle type pin, it should be noted that this style pin was characteristic of medal firms in Pforzheim during the period.

266

The badge was instituted by the head of the National Socialist Riding Corps (Nationalsozialistisches Reiterkorps - NSRK), SA-Obergruppenführer Litzmann. To qualify for the award, the intended recipient must:

a. have served one year as an officer in the NSRK, or

b. have passed the riding and horse-drawn vehicle proficiency test with a capability of instructing others in horsemanship, and

d. have been awarded the SA Sport badge.

The 53mm badge was designed by Paul Casberg, and was worn on the lower left breast. No other riding badge was worn when this badge was being worn.

The obverse of the badge shows a mounted SA man surrounded by an oakleaf wreath with the SA insignia at the base. On the reverse is the issue serial number, the manufacturer's logo, and the initials of the designer, Paul Casberg.

In regard to the bronze example, it is possible that the award was expanded to include a bronze, silver and gold class. However, there is no documentation to support this.

Mohawk Arms

Reverse of the standard silver badge made by the same firm.

BADGE FOR THE CARE OF HORSES
(Deutsches Pferdepflegerabzeichen)

The last badge to be instituted by the Federation was the German Badge for the Care of Horses (Deutsches Pferdepflegerabzeichen), founded in 1937. The badge was probably designed by W. Heitinger, and measured 44mm. It was awarded in three grades:

a. The 3rd Class (bronze) required:

(1) At least ten years employment at the same stable, stud or other equestrian establishment, or

(2)   For breeders, obtaining five commendations for good care and grooming from remount or stallion markets, or

(3)   Winning at least 10 first place awards at public tournaments or races, or

(4)   For outstanding achievement in the improvement of stock.

b.   The 2nd Class (silver) required:

(1)   At least fifteen years employment at the same stable, stud or other equestrian establishment, or

(2)   For breeders, obtaining ten commendations for good care and grooming from remount or stallion markets, or

(3)   Winning at least 20 first place awards at public tournaments or races, or

(4)   Having already obtained the badge in bronze, further demonstrated achievement in the improvement of stock.

c.   The 1st Class (gold) required:

Maroon-colored case for the Golden Badge for the Care of Horses.

Gold badge with miniature stickpin.

Reverse

(1)   At least twenty years employment at the same stable, stud or other equestrian establishment, or

(2)   For breeders, obtaining fifteen commendations for good care and grooming from remount or stallion markets, or

(3)   Winning at least fifteen horse shows, or

(4)   Winning at least 30 first place awards at public tournaments or races.

The round badge had an oakleaf wreath with a Roman "R" at the base surrounding a trotting horse being led by a running man.   The reverse bore the manufacturer's logo around the wreath.   It was presented in a cardboard presentation box containing the badge and a stickpin miniature.   The badge was worn on the lower left breast when appropriate, while the stickpin was worn, in the absence of the badge, on the left lapel.   An award document accompanied the award.

An identical badge, but without the "R", was awarded by the Central Commission for Testing Thoroughbreds from 1933 until the introduction of the National Federation badge.

A plaque for Outstanding Achievements in Equestrian Care and Handling was also awarded, but the exact criteria for award are not known.   This was also presented in bronze, silver or gold.   The rectangular plaque bore a copy of the badge for the

Plaque for Outstanding Achievement in gold

Care of Horses.   At the top of the plaque was the inscription 'Reichsverband für Zucht und Prüfung Deutschen Warmbluts' (National Federation for the Breeding and Testing of German Thoroughbreds), and at the bottom "Für hervorrangende Leistungen in Pferdepflege und Haltung" (For Outstanding Achievements in the Care and Handling of Horses).   An identical plaque was also awarded by the Central Commission, but the badge had no "R" at the base of the wreath, and the inscription read "Zentralkommission für Pferdeleistungsprüfungen" (Central Commission for Horse Achievement Testing) and "Für hervorragende Leistungen in Pferdepflege und Haltung" (For Outstanding Achievements in the Care and Handling of Horses).

Many badges for the Care of Horses found in collections are, in fact, not the badge, but the badge portion of the plaque that has been removed.   This is evident from the prongs on the reverse (rather than the clasp).

The precise number of awards rendered is not known, but by virtue of the criteria, it must rank among the rarest of badges.

𝔜outh Awards

GOLDEN LEADER'S SPORTS BADGE
(Das Goldene Führer-Sportabzeichen)

Reichsjugendführer Baldur von Schirach decreed on 18 January 1937 that all Hitler Youth leaders from the rank of Fähnlein to Gefolgschaftsführer would be required to annually pass a decathelon test consisting of: (a) 1000 meter sprint, (b) 1000 meter run, (c) high jump, (d) long jump, (e) shot put, (f) putting the weight, (g) 300 meter swim, (h) marksman qualification, both supported and unsupported, and (i) road march with full pack.

The Golden Leader's Sport badge (das Goldene Führer-Sportabzeichen) was instituted by von Schirach on 15 May 1938 to be awarded annually to the high scorers in the decathelon. In order to qualify, the competitor must have received the HJ Proficiency badge in silver, and must have met the standards for award in the decathelon. Two standards of grades existed based on the age of the competitor, but that age distinction is not known. Step A required an accumulation of 7,500 points, while Step B (presumably the older group) required a total of 6,500 to be achieved over the two day test. There was no limitation placed on the number of recipients, providing they met the necessary qualifications.

The first award was presented at Nürnberg at the Party Rally in 1938. No awards were rendered after 1943. An estimated 11,000 badges were presented during this period.

Obverse   **Reverse**

Unidentified Hitler Youth Leader wears the **Golden Leader's Sports badge** on the right breast pocket. Later regulations specified that the badge would be worn on the left breast pocket.

This Golden Leader's Badge carries a serial number rather than the 'A' or 'B' designation.

Early regulations were unclear as to where the badge was to be worn, and, as a result, most were worn on the right breast pocket. In 1942, regulations specified that the badge was to be worn on the left breast pocket.

The gold badge featured the Hitler Youth Proficiency badge on a round dark blue enamel field surrounded by a gold laurel wreath. The reverse bore either the serial number of the award or the designation 'A' or 'B', determined by the accumulation of points. Also on the reverse was the RZM/manufacturer's logo. The badge measured 51mm high by 37mm wide.

HITLER YOUTH PROFICIENCY BADGE
(Leistungsabzeichen der Hitler Jugend)

Reichsjugendführer von Schirach instituted a badge in June 1934 to serve as an incentive to the growing membership of the Hitler Youth to improve their physical and ideological proficiency.

All members of the HJ organizations were issued a 'Leistungsbuch' (qualification book) so that their achievements might be recorded and certified.   A book was given to the boys of the DJ-HJ with one set of grading standards, and another was given to the girls of the JM-BDM with a different set of standards.

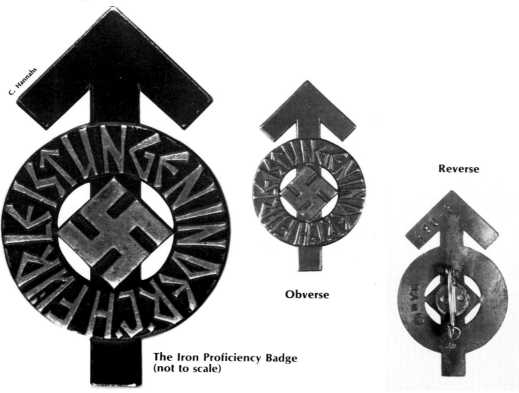

Reverse

Obverse

C. Hannahs

The Iron Proficiency Badge
(not to scale)

The Hitler Youth Proficiency badge awarded to boys consisted of a swastika encircled by the wording "Für Leistungen in der HJ" (For Proficiency in the HJ) in sham runic script.   This is superimposed on a runic 'T' or 'Tyr-Rune'.   The badge measured 51mm high by 30mm wide.   The grades of the award were as follows:

    a.   Iron (Class A, B and C).   Awarded to members of the HJ, this badge was restricted to boys 15 years old.   This is the standard pattern badge painted black with the swastika and inscription in silver tones.[1]   The reverse bore the serial number of the award, and was recorded in the Leistungsbuch.   This award was not intended as an interim award for the DJ.

A young Hitler Youth member is inspected by a visiting foreign delegation under the close supervision of two Hitler Youth Leaders. The boy wears the silver HJ Proficiency badge on his right breast pocket. Regulations later prescribed that it be worn on the left breast pocket.

b. Bronze (Class A, B and C). This badge was awarded to 16 year old male members of the Hitler Youth. The reverse is serial numbered. By the end of 1943, a total of 103,061 awards had been authorized.

c. Silver (aluminum) (Class A, B, and C). A total of 217,093 awards had been presented to 17 year old male HJ members by the end of 1943. The reverse is serial numbered.

Some badges bore the A, B or C designation of the proficiency test taken, but most were without this designation as an entry in the proficiency book usually sufficed for this purpose.

A three-part test was administered, consisting of (a) athletics and gymnastics, (b) field exercises, and (c) political knowledge. Within these tests were degrees of proficiency which resulted in a Class A, B or C ultimately being awarded. A person receiving a Class C award could be tested at a later date to qualify for a higher award. It was not necessary to progress from a Class C rating to a higher rating since the higher class included the proficiency degree of the lower.

The badge was worn by members of the HJ, SA, SS, RAD and the military on their uniform. Early regulations were unclear as to where the award would be worn; it was

---

[1] *Organisationsbuch der NSDAP*, 1943 edition

A miniature version of the HJ Proficiency badge measuring 19mm could be purchased for RM 25, and was worn on the left lapel of the civilian clothes.

Miniature to exact scale

Cloth version of the HJ Proficiency badge for the athletic shirt. Tan on white (illustration) represented the Bronze award; gray on black represented the Silver award. Black on white was for Iron. The cloth 'badge' was worn on the lower left breast.

usually worn on the right side. However, later regulations specified that it would be worn on the left breast pocket. A miniature version was authorized for wear on the lapel of civilian clothes. A cloth version was worn on the athletic shirt.

GERMAN YOUTH PROFICIENCY BADGE
(Deutsches Jugend-Leistungsabzeichen)

The Leistungsabzeichen des Deutschen Jungvolks(Proficiency Badge of the German Young People - the official designation of the badge) was instituted by von Schirach on 26 September 1935 to be awarded to boys between the ages of 10 and 14 who were members of the German Youth (DJ).

A different degree of testing was required depending on the age of the boy involved. However, the badge was not awarded until the recipient reached the age of 12. A single award in dull gray metal was presented upon successful testing in (a) general academics (b) athletics (c) field exercises (d) shooting.

A total of 152,600 awards was made before awards ceased in 1944. The badge was worn on the left breast pocket, on the lower left breast in cloth on the athletic shirt, and on the left lapel for the metal miniature.

The badge took the design of the runic 'S' or Sigrune, in the center of which was a swastika encircled with the inscription "Für Leistungen im D.J." (For Proficiency in the D.J.) in simulated runic letters. It measured 45mm high by 23mm wide.

Obverse	Reverse

LEAGUE OF GERMAN GIRLS PROFICIENCY CLASP
(Bund Deutscher Mädel Leistungsabzeichen)

A proficiency clasp for members of the Bund Deutscher Mädel (BDM - League of German Girls) was instituted by von Schirach on 28 April 1934. It was to be awarded to girls between the ages of 14 and 21 who had successfully passed tests in first aid,

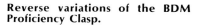
Reverse variations of the BDM Proficiency Clasp.

nursing, homecraft, athletics, and political ideology during a twelve month period. Award was to be in two classes - bronze and silver; the classes were probably based on the recipient's age. Within each class were three subdivisions, Grades A, B and C, which were awarded depending on the degree of proficiency attained in the tests.

The clasp consisted of the letters 'BDM' inside a rectangular frame with a 29mm length of ribbon (red, white, red) in the background. On the reverse was the RZM logo, the grade designation, and the serial number of the award. The metal portion was either bronze or silver, depending on the class of the award. The clasp was worn on the left breast of the BDM uniform. An estimated 115,000 awards in bronze were presented. Award figures for the silver class are not known.

YOUNG GIRLS PROFICIENCY CLASP
(Jungmädel Leistungsabzeichen)

Girls between the ages of 10 and 14 belonged to the Jungmädel (JM - Young Girls). A proficiency clasp was instituted, probably at the same time as the BDM clasp on 28 April 1934, to be awarded for excellence in tests similar to the BDM tests, but with a lower grade cut-off. The tests had to be completed within a twelve month period.

Only one class existed - silver. The badge or clasp consisted of the letters 'JM' in a 21mm long frame with a red ribbon background. The reverse bore the serial number of the award. Approximately 58,000 awards were rendered.

The clasp was worn on the upper left breast of the JM uniform.

Award of the badge was not made until the girl reached the age of 12.

278

The above girls are shown wearing the BDM Proficiency Clasp while attending the BDM Leadership School.

HITLER YOUTH SHOOTING AWARDS
(HJ-Schiessauszeichnungen)

Starting in 1936 a series of marksmanship qualification badges were instituted by Reichsjugendführer Baldur von Schirach in an effort to stimulate competitive shooting among members of the Hitler Youth and German Youth. Competitive shooting was intended to be as much a form of pre-military training as a sports exercise, and was but one of many military exercises integrated into the HJ curriculum. Authorized recipients were permitted to wear the badge on the left breast pocket of their uniform.[2] The qualifications were achieved with small bore rifles only, and were as follows:

---

[2] *It appears that there was some early confusion concerning the manner of wear as some recipients wore the badge on the right breast pocket.*

Marksman: A 21mm round enamel badge was awarded following its institution late in 1936 to HJ members over 16 years of age who had qualified by shooting well (five rounds in the prone position with the rifle supported; five rounds in the prone position without support; five rounds in an unsupported kneeling position).   The obverse of the badge was black enamel with four silver target rings.   In the center was the HJ diamond in silver and enamel with two crossed silver rifles.   The reverse bore the RZM and manufacturer's logo.   By the end of 1943 a total of 273,545 badges had been awarded.

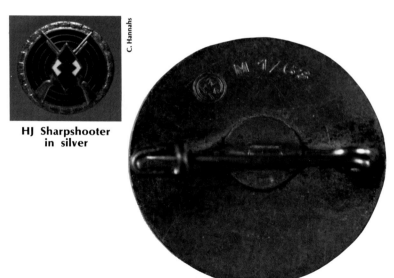

HJ Marksman

Sharpshooter: Same badge as above, but with the addition of a 2mm silver oakleaf wreath around the outer edge.   This badge was instituted in 1938, and by the end of 1943 a total of 31,904 badges had been awarded.   Qualification for the badge consisted of firing ten rounds each in the prone supported, prone unsupported, kneeling and standing positions.

**HJ Sharpshooter
in silver**

Master Shooter: Instituted on 3 December 1941, the badge was identical to the Sharpshooter badge except that all the metal parts were in gold.   Recipients of this badge were classified as 'champions'.   To qualify, ten shots were fired from the prone unsupported, prone supported, kneeling and standing positions, but the required points were increased.   By the end of 1943, a total of 852 badges had been awarded.

DJ Shooting award: Persons under 16 years of age who were members of the Deutsches Jungvolk(German Young People - DJ) were eligible to compete. Those receiving the award were given a badge consisting of a 21mm round black enamel badge with four silver target rings in the center of which was the DJ Sigrune(runic S) on two silver crossed rifles, and the letters 'D' and 'J' in white enamel. Pneumatic rifles were used for qualification. A total of 580,872 awards were rendered by the end of 1943. The exact date of institution is not certain, but it is believed to have been late in 1936.

C. Hannahs

DJ Shooting award

Late production awards were produced from zinc, and as a result, it was not unusual for the silver plating to discolor, leaving a dull gray finish.

Bud Hasher

The Hitler Youth Leader in the center and the one on the left wear the HJ Marksman award on the right breast pocket below their HJ Proficiency award.

NATIONAL LEADER'S SCHOOL BREAST INSIGNIA
(Reichs-Führer-Schule Abzeichen)

Hitler Youth Leaders who were selected to attend the Reichs-Führer-Schule, and who successfully completed the course were authorized to wear the insignia of the Reichs-Führer-Schule (RFS).   This was not intended to be an award, but was merely a 'graduate's badge' similar to the famous 'Tyr-Rune'.

The insignia was in cloth form only - silver bullion with black outline with the initials 'RFS' in the center on a brown, tan or black background.   It was worn over the right breast pocket of all Hitler Youth uniforms.

The insignia is believed to have been created in 1935, and served as an incentive to aspiring Youth Leaders.

It is shown here simply for the reader's interest.

The Hitler Youth Leader in the center wears the Reichs-Führer-Schule insignia over his right breast pocket.

DECORATION OF THE HIGH COMMAND OF THE HITLER YOUTH
FOR DISTINGUISHED FOREIGNERS
(Ehrenzeichen der Reichsjugendführung der HJ für Verdiente Ausländer)

A special badge was created by the Hitler Youth leadership branch in 1941 for award to non-Germans in recognition of services on behalf of European youth. More precise details are not known.

The silver and enamel badge measured 34mm high and 32mm across the eagle's outstretched wings. It was worn on the lower left breast.

The basic badge was a white enamel oval with a brown enamel border with the inscription 'Hitler Jugend' in gold. Affixed to the enamel portion was a silver eagle with outstretched wings clasping silver oakleaves and the insigne of the Hitler Youth in red, black and white enamel.

The reverse is plain with a horizontal brooch-type pin and three rivets which secure the eagle device.

D. Leach

| Obverse | Reverse |

CLASP OF THE GERMAN YOUTH CHAMPION
(Nadel des Deutschen Jugendmeisters)

Reichsjugendführer Axmann instituted awards in 1942 to recognize winners (either male or female) in the year-round indoor and outdoor sports competitions. The award came in three classes:

a. Golden Clasp of the German Youth Champion (Goldene Nadel des Deutschen Jugendmeisters): A 29mm round gold award presented to the 1st place winner in any individual or team national competition. The Hitler Youth diamond emblem in enamel surmounted the date of award on a blue enamel field. The outer edge was composed of laurel leaves and had the inscription 'Jugendmeister' (Youth Champion) at the bottom.

b. Clasp for 2nd Place Winner (Nadel für zweiten Sieger): Similar to the golden clasp, except that the outer edge had an oakleaf wreath with the inscription

283

Golden Clasp

**Clasp for 2nd Place
Winner**

'Kampfspiele' (Competitive Games).   The base metal was silver.   It was presented to the individual or team placing second in a competition.

c.   Clasp for 3rd Place Winner (Nadel für dritten Sieger):   This was identical to the silver clasp, except that it was finished in bronze.   This clasp was awarded to the third place individual or team.

The clasp was worn on the left breast pocket.   Even though each award was dated for the year of the competition, it could be worn permanently.

HONOR BADGE OF THE NATIONAL CHAMPIONS
(Ehrennadel der Reichssieger)

A badge in bronze (third place), silver (second place) and gold (first place) was established at the same time as the clasp of the German Youth Champions.   This ranked below these awards either because there were too few competitors to warrant a higher award, or because all competitors were below the age of 16.

Even though the badge was dated, it was permitted to be worn permanently.   It was worn on the left breast pocket.

The badge measured 26mm and had the base color of the level of award (bronze, silver or gold) with a blue enamel background.   The center motif was the Hitler Youth emblem surmounting the date, which was surrounded by an oakleaf wreath with the inscription 'Reichssieger' at the bottom.

N.S.F.K. AERO-MODELLING PROFICIENCY BADGE
(NSFK Modelflugleistungsabzeichen)

A concerted effort was made to stimulate interest in flying and aeronautics among the youth of Germany, for it was this group that would eventually furnish Hitler with most of his future combat pilots. The Hitler Youth established special modelling groups (Modellfluggruppen) open to members of the Hitler Youth and German Youth. These groups were controlled by members of the NSFK, and were often supervised in their competitions by representatives of the Air Force.

Model competitions were often held in the fields of motor-driven and glider aircraft. Boys brought the aircraft that they had built to a large hilly meadow, and flew them in competitions based on the length of the flight, maneuvers, etc. A qualification badge in three grades was the prize that awaited successful modelers:

a. Grade 'A' (A-Prüfung): The 'A' badge (A-Abzeichen) was a round cloth badge depicting a glider within two concentric circles. The glider, circles and cloud representations were finished in white thread on blue-gray backing. To earn this badge it was necessary for the entrant to understand the principles of flight, make at least 30 test flights with his model, and successfully pass five test flights from launch to landing.

Grade 'A'

b. Grade 'B' (B-Prüfung): The 'B' badge (B-Abzeichen) was oval in shape, and showed a glider diving into a cloud. This was surrounded by an oakleaf wreath with a swastika at the bottom. The badge was executed in matte-yellow on a blue-gray background. To earn this badge the competitor had to perform maneuvers with his model, causing his plane to make a 90° and a 360° turn during five tests out of 20 flights.

c. Grade 'C' (C-Prüfung): The design of the 'C' badge (C-Abzeichen) was identical to that of the 'B', except that it was fabricated in aluminum wire on a blue-gray background. It was necessary to have obtained the 'A' and 'B' badges before the competition for this award could be entered. The modeler was required to perform

Grade 'C'

maneuvers and to keep his model aloft for a period of one-half hour during the course of 20 test flights.

The date of introduction of the awards is not known. Specifications for award were established by the NSFK, and bestowal was rigidly supervised by that organization.

Another badge is illustrated here for which there is no specific information available. It is similar in design to the 'B' and 'C' Grade badges except that it is round rather than oval, and lacks the swastika at the bottom. This metal award may have been introduced at a later date, or it may represent an award for a particular modelling competition, but this is mere speculation. The badge measures 39mm, and has a bronze color. The pin on the reverse indicates that it was worn on the uniform jacket. The reverse bears the design patent number at the top and a serial number at the bottom. An identical miniature measuring 20mm also bore the serial number.

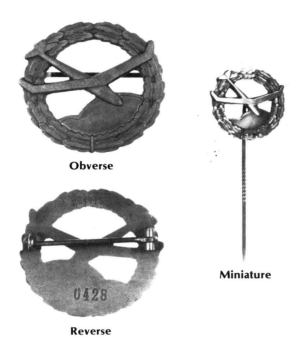

Obverse

Miniature

Reverse

HITLER YOUTH EXPERT SKIER BADGE
(HJ Skiführerabzeichen)

The specific criteria for award of the Hitler Youth Expert Skier badge are not known, but it is probable that some sort of rigid alpine skier test was taken to earn the award. This badge is believed to be a qualification badge rather than an award for achievement. It is probable that Hitler Youth Ski Instructors were given it as a mark of qualification upon passing their tests prior to becoming recognized instructors. It is doubtful that this badge was open to the entire HJ membership.

One source places the date of institution as late 1933 or early 1934, but this cannot be confirmed. No additional information is available concerning the manner of wear, etc. However, it is assumed that the badge was worn on the left breast or centered on the chest of the ski uniform. The badge was attached to the uniform by two horizontal clasp pins.

The old (tarnished appearance) silver badge bears the Hitler Youth enamel emblem centered on a single large edelweiss flower surmounting two crossed skis and mounted on an outer circle bearing the inscription 'Ski-HJ-Führer'. The circle measures

Members of the N.S.F.K., Luftwaffe, and Hitler Youth inspect the glider of a Hitler ›uth entrant in the aero-model competition. Note the glider's qualification badge ›rn on the pocket of the Hitler Youth Leader.

60mm, and the ends of the skis project beyond this, making it the largest of the Hitler Youth badges. The reverse bears the patent pending mark and the manufacturer's logo (Wittmann, München).

Obverse

Reverse

Obverse

Reverse

Second Place award medal for the Reich Youth competition for 1936.   The medal is silver suspended from a yellow ribbon with white stripes.

Non-Reich Level Awards

HERMANN GÖRING COMMEMORATIVE MEDAL OF THE GERMAN ACADEMY FOR AERONAUTICAL RESEARCH
(Hermann-Göring-Denkmünze der Deutschen Akademie der Luftfahrtforschung)

On 21 January 1938, the same date as the founding of the German Academy for Aeronautical Research (Die deutsche Akademie der Luftfahrtforschung) by Hermann Göring, a commemorative medal was established. It was designated the 'Hermann Göring Commemorative Medal of the German Academy for Aeronautical Research' (Die Hermann-Göring-Denkmünze der Deutschen Akademie der Luftfahrtforschung). It was approved for award, given in the name of, and personally presented by the President of the Academy, Hermann Göring. It was to be awarded to those persons, both German and non-German, who had made a significant contribution to the advancement of aeronautical research. Those persons selected to receive the medal automatically received membership in the Academy.

Membership in the Academy was very restricted, and the commemorative medal was also regarded as a badge of membership. As of 1 March 1942, total membership numbered 150 persons, with another eleven being introduced into the ranks during the remainder of 1942. Among these new members was Reich Minister Albert Speer (1 September 1942), who was accorded honorary membership.

The commemorative medal took the form of a stylized eagle clutching a swastika (similar to that of the Luftwaffe Pilot's badge), surrounded by an angular oakleaf wreath suspended from three oakleaves. The medal took the following forms:

a.   The highest class was worn suspended from a chain of office; this gold medal was worn only by the President of the Academy and members of the Presidium.

b.   The Golden Badge of the Academy, which was worn by Honorary Members and Regular Members of the Academy.

c.   The Silver Badge of the Academy, which was worn by Sponsoring Members.

d.   The Bronze Badge of the Academy, which was worn by Corresponding Members.

The decoration came in two sizes - large (Grosses Abzeichen) and small (Kleines Abzeichen). Except in the case of the chain of office, the large size was worn in pin-back form on the left breast pocket during formal occasions. The miniature version,

Golden miniature worn by members of the Praesidium and Honorary Members on other than formal occasions. (Not to scale)

Gary L. Walker Museum Collection

Reverse of the golden miniature (not to scale)

which measured 64mm high (with suspension), was worn on the left lapel suspended by a needle pin, at the discretion of the member.[1]

The Academy charter specified that the commemorative medal remained the property of the Academy, and was to be returned upon the death of the recipient.

The piece was presented with an award document personally signed by Göring.

---

[1]*A sincere debt of gratitude is owed to Mr. Bill Stump for providing the documentation Jahrbuch der Deutschen Akademie der Luftfahrtforschung for the years 1938/39 to 1942/43, from which this information is drawn.*

A visiting Italian dignitary listens intently to Göring. He has been awarded numerous German decorations including the Pilot/Observer badge with diamonds, the Grand Cross to the Eagle Order with and without swords, and the miniature version of the Hermann Göring Commemorative Medal of the German Academy for Aeronautical Research. Note that the latter decoration takes the highest precedence.

The reverse of the miniature (Nadel) bore the manufacturer's logo, serial number and silver content number. The reverse of the chain of office or the badge have not been observed to allow description.

It should be noted that any reference to the above described medal and the membership badge of the Academy actually refers to a single medal - the commemorative medal.

LONG SERVICE AND ACHIEVEMENT AWARDS OF THE NATIONAL FOOD ESTATE
(Leistungs- und Dienstauszeichnungen für den Reichsnährstand)

As virtually every facet of German life came under the control of the NSDAP, more incentives were created to propound the merits of the various Nazi-run organizations. Unofficial awards were established to motivate the sometimes less-than-willing members, and to capitalize on the propaganda value that was to be derived from related award ceremonies. Such was the case with the National Food Estate (Reichsnährstand), the organization created in September 1933 by Walter Darré,

Walter Darré

which incorporated all functions related to food producing. In December 1936, Darré instituted a series of long service awards to recognize dedicated service in the furtherance of food production for Germany. Surprisingly, these long service awards were not struck (or presented) on a national level, but were designed (and awarded) at the discretion of the individual German states (Gau). Some degree of uniformity was present in that the emblem of the Reichsnährstand was incorporated into the design, and the metal used to designate service time did remain uniform, e.g.

10 Years Service: plated alloy (same as 20 Years Service)

20 Years Service: iron

30 Years Service: bronze

40 Years Service: silver

50 Years Service: gold

The motto of the Reichsnährstand, 'Blut und Boden' (Blood and Earth), which was an integral part of the organization's emblem, became a rallying cry for the production of greater quantities of food once the war broke out.

The following are a few representative examples of the various state-designed awards which recognized service and achievement:

East Prussia (Ostpreussen): The obverse, which bears the inscription 'Landesbauernschaft Ostpreussen' (State Peasants Group East Prussia), is identical for all service awards presented by this state. The reverse is basically the same, with only

295

Obverse   **Reverse**

the number of the years of service changing.   These awards were produced in a medal form which measured 35mm.   Awards made to men were suspended by a green ribbon, while those made to women were suspended from a green bow.   Additionally, a metal ring (women) or bar (men) was affixed to the ribbon, and corresponded to the grade of the medal, e.g., bronze for 30 years, silver for 40 years, etc.

Rhineland: Service awards for the Rhineland were in the form of pin-back badges rather than medals, but interestingly enough the reverse was struck with a year designation and other design patterns.   The obverse did not bear a state designation, but employed the basic Reichsnährstand design with the addition of the inscription 'Für treue Gefolgschaft' (For Loyal Membership).   The reverse bore the inscription 'Landesbauernschaft Rheinland für (year designation of the award) Jahre Pflicht u. Treue' (State Peasants Group Rhineland for (-) years duty and loyalty).   The badge measured 34mm.

Obverse   **Reverse**

In addition to the service awards, achievement awards and special category awards were created to be awarded to members of the Reichsnährstand. These awards were established to recognize the accomplishments of the member in a particular field of endeavor or competition. The following are but a few of the various incentive awards that were presented:

Rhineland Achievement Award for Agriculture: This gold medal (awarded without a ribbon suspension) bears the inscription 'Für Leistungen im Ackerbau' (For Achievement in Agriculture) surrounded by a wreath of agricultural products on the reverse.

Obverse   **Reverse**

The presentation case for this award was finished in a mahogany-colored grain pattern. There was no insignia on the top of the lid. The inner lid was finished in purple satin, while the lower section was finished in dark blue velvet.

1938 National Food Estate National Competition Award for Milk and Milk Products: Shown here is the bronze award for achievement in the 1938 national competition. This particular award was given for excellence in the preparation of milk cheese. It measured 60mm, and was presented in a black hard case bearing the emblem of the National Food Estate in silver on the lid. The inner lid of the case was white satin, while the lower compartmented section was dark blue velvet.

Obverse

Reverse

Case for the Competition Award for Milk and Milk Products.

Special Award for the Production of Farm Stock: This special award was presented by the National Food Estate for achievement in the raising of farm animals. The 42mm round silver medallion bore the inscription 'Für Landwirtschaftliche Leistungen' surrounded by a wreath of food products on the reverse. The obverse bore the figure of Germania surrounded by various farm symbols. The edge bears the silver content designation '835'. It was presented in a black hard case with a gold national emblem embossed on a vaulted lid. The interior of the lid was white satin, while the compartmented lower section was finished in purple velvet.

Obverse   Reverse

FIRE BRIGADE DECORATION (PRUSSIA)

The Prussian Minister of the interior instituted a Prussian state decoration on 21 December 1933 for meritorious service in the Prussian Fire Brigade. The award was in the form of an oval measuring 42mm high and 29mm wide, and was struck in silver by the Prussian mint. It was awarded by the Prussian Minister of the Interior following recommendation from the Prussian Chief of Police, and was given in recognition of proven bravery in the line of duty or for 25 years loyal service in the Fire Brigade.

The badge shows a fireman sounding the alarm and holding a fire hose. On his chest is the Prussian eagle. Below is a burning house. Around the outer edge of the

The presentation case is a two-piece hinged hard case with simulated black leather exterior. The interior of the upper portion is white satin, while the lower portion is light blue velvet.

badge is the inscription 'Für Verdienste um das Feuerlöschwesen' (For Service n the Fire Brigade) with a swastika at the bottom.

The reverse of the badge has the legend 'Silber 900 Fein' and 'Preuss. Staatsmünze' (Prussian State Mint).

The award was superseded by the Fire Brigade decoration, which was instituted by the German Federal government on 22 December 1936.

FIRE BRIGADE MEDAL OF MERIT (HANOVER)

The Medal of Merit of the Fire Brigade for the State of Hanover was instituted on 26 April 1934. It was to be awarded for loyal service in the Hanover Fire Brigade. This silver medal was worn suspended from a yellow and white ribbon (the colors for the State of Hanover).

The obverse of the 29mm medal bore the inscription 'Für Verdienste um das Feuerlöschwesen' (For Service in the Fire Brigade) surrounding a fire helmet with small swastika insigne. The reverse had the inscription 'Feuerwehr-Verband für die Provinz Hanover. Gegr. 26.7.1868' (Fire Brigade Association for the Province of Hanover, Founded 26. 7. 1868) surrounding a prancing horse, the state symbol of Hanover.

This award was superseded by the national Fire Brigade decoration instituted on 22 December 1936.

Obverse   **Reverse**

MEDAL FOR LOYAL WORK (EAST THURINGIA)

Another of the state awards was the Medal for Loyal Work instituted by the East Thuringian Chamber of Industry and Commerce. The medal was awarded in three classes - bronze, silver and gold - in recognition of a contribution made to labor. The obverse of the medal shows management shaking hands with labor, and bears the inscription 'Arbeit Adelt' (Labor Enobles), which later became the official motto of the RAD. The reverse has a swastika in the center over the inscription 'Für Treue in der Arbeit' (For Loyalty in Work). Around the outer edge is the inscription 'Ostthüring. Industrie und Handels-Kammer' (East Thuringian Chamber of Industry and Commerce). The medal, which was designed by a Herrn Eyermann, is suspended from a white and red ribbon, which are the state colors of Thuringia.

Obverse   **Reverse**   301

HONOR BADGE FOR MEMBERS OF THE NATIONAL SENATE OF CULTURE
(Ehrenplakette für die Mitglieder des Reichs-Kultur-Senats)

The first award of the Honor Badge for Members of the National Senate of Culture was made on 28 November 1936, when it was presented to 125 members of the Senate. The badge, which was awarded to the entire membership, recognized the members' contributions on behalf of cultural endeavor.

The National Chamber of Culture (Reichskulturkammer) was established by law on 22 September 1933. Its purpose was to act as a coordinating point for the various cultural, and culturally-related areas: art, music, theater, films, literature, press and radio. The ultimate control of the Chamber was vested in the Minister of Propaganda, Dr. Joseph Goebbels, but it was nominally exercised by the National Senate of Culture (Reichskultursenat). The Senate, established on 15 November 1935, was the governing body of the Chamber, and was composed of indivudals connected with the various arts, or those who had 'contributed' to the advancement of German culture. Goebbels had long controlled the communications media. The establishment of the Chamber provided an opportunity for him to extend his control still further, and to use various art forms to convey his propaganda themes.

A badge to honor the men of the Senate was designed by Professor Richard Klein. It measured 44mm wide by 56mm high, and was basically oval in shape. A black eagle surmounting a gold Ionic column over a swastika was the central design of the badge. Arched about this was the inscription 'Reichskultursenat'. The background of the badge was cream colored enamel. Around the outer perimeter was a gold border coming to a series of points. It was worn on the lower left breast, and was authorized for wear on either the uniform or civilian dress.

Obverse

Reverse

B. Regnemer

Reichsbank President Walther Funk wears the Badge of Honor for members of the National Senate of Culture below the Golden Party Badge.

A stickpin was authorized for wear on the left lapel on occasions when the wear of decorations on civilian clothes was not appropriate. The silver miniature differed slightly from the badge in that the initials 'R.K.S.' were arched above the eagle's head rather than the entire title being spelled out.

Interestingly, members of the National Chamber of Culture were authorized to wear a similar stickpin. This was only a mark of recognition for members of the Chamber, and was not considered to be a badge of honor. Authorized for wear in April 1937, the stickpin retained the basic design of the National Senate of Culture, but the initials 'R.K.S.' were replaced by the initials 'R.K.K.', which were positioned below the swastika rather than above the eagle's head.

The reverse of the badge bore the manufacturer's designation and the silver content number - ('Deschler München Silber 900').

There is no accurate estimate of the number of badges actually awarded. It is doubtful that the membership of the Senate underwent very many changes, which limited the requirement for badges. It is probable that less than 300 badges were awarded, but this figure is purely speculative.

ANHALT LABOR SERVICE COMMEMORATIVE BADGE
(Anhaltisches Arbeitsdienst-Erinnerungsabzeichen)

Unemployment in Germany was enormous during the Depression years, and became a point of contention between the various political factions. As early as 1928, an ardent Nazi named Konstantin Hierl hit on the idea of a national labor service which would help to bring Germany out of the Depression. In June 1931, Brüning's Weimar government passed an emergency decree creating a voluntary labor service, and in so doing attempted to weaken Hitler's political platform concerning unemployment.

The Nazis immediately entered the program, which they in fact had created, in an effort to gain control over the workers. Nazi control was virtually complete in the state of Anhalt, where the National Socialist Labor Service spread rapidly throughout the state. Anhalt set the example for other German states; the state was quick to point to the Labor Service's Nazi leadership as a source of its success.

The state of Anhalt instituted a commemorative badge to be awarded to members of the Anhalt Labor Service (Anhalt Arbeitsdienst - AAD) on 30 September 1933. The badge was intended to recognize Anhalt as the location of the first state labor service, and, in effect, as the birthplace of the National Labor Service (Reichsarbeitsdienst). The badge was established in bronze, silver and gold, and was awarded

Obverse	Reverse
	The reverse is void of any markings.

1st Pattern

in two nearly identical patterns.[2] The first pattern had a 23mm round disc in the center of a 33mm swastika. The disc bore the letters 'AAD' (Anhalt Arbeitsdienst) over the date '1932'. This badge was awarded to all persons who had served at least 20 months with the Anhalt Labor Service or in the first Nazi labor camp at Hammerstein before 1 January 1933. The second pattern was identical in design, but omitted the

[2]*Uniformen-Markt* 7/1.4.1941.

Reichsarbeitsführer Konstantin Hierl speaks with a RAD section leader. Hierl and a member of his staff to his rear both wear the Anhalt Labor Service Commemorative badge.

year date. This badge was awarded to those members who had served between 1 January 1933 and 31 July 1935. The grade of the award depended on the length of service involved and the significance of the special service rendered the labor service.

The Anhalt Labor Service Commemorative badge only received semi-official recognition when it was allowed to be worn on the RAD uniform. However, it never received official recognition as a national award. The badge was worn on the left breast pocket.

BADGE OF THE GERMAN LIFE SAVING ASSOCIATION
(Abzeichen der Deutschen Lebensrettungsgesellschaft - DLRG)

The German Life Saving Association was founded in 1913, and was an off-shoot of the German Swimming League. Its avowed purpose was to train persons in water safety.

On 25 September 1933, the President of the DLRG placed his organization under the overall control of the Reich Sports Leader, and a series of awards was instituted corresponding to various degrees of proficiency.

The first level of proficiency resulted in the award of the 'Grundschein', or basic certificate, and a bronze lapel pin depicting the emblem of the DLRG, with the word 'Grundschein'. The second level was the 'Prüfungsschein' or test certificate. Here the qualification tests became more rigorous, and resulted in the award of a certificate and a silver lapel pin identical in design, but bearing the word 'Prüfungsschein'. The highest level of proficiency resulted in the award of the 'Lehrschein', or instructor's

305

certificate, which enabled the recipient to wear a silver lapel pin.[3]   In addition to the qualification badges, all members of the DLRG were authorized to wear the organization's emblem on their athletic uniform.

DLRG Membership insignia worn on the athletic uniform.   The letters are black, the eagle green, and the water blue.

DLRG Lifesaving badge. This particular specimen was made by the Assmann firm, and besides bearing the manufacturer's logo, it is serial numbered.

A badge was awarded for saving the life of an endangered person in the water.   Presentation was made by the President of the DLRG, Georg Har.   Inasmuch as the purpose of the DLRG was to train persons in water lifesaving, such an act by qualified members did not merit the award of the   Lifesaving   Medal or Medallion.   Thus, the organization recognized heroism by its own members by presenting them a silver oval badge measuring 57mm wide by 40mm high.   It depicted a partially flying eagle with its feet on the ground - symbolic of the earth-water relationship.   The initials 'DLRG' rested on the waves of the water.   The entire badge was encircled by an oakleaf wreath.   The badge was worn on the lower left breast.

[3]*Nationalsozialistischer Lehrerbund Jahrbuch 1935.*

The 'Leistungsschein' and 'Grundschein' lapel pin for wear on civilian clothes.

MERIT BADGE OF THE NSKOV

The title of 'Merit Badge of the National Socialist War Disabled Welfare Organization' (NS Kriegsopferversorgung - NSKOV) is used with reservation, and for want of a more definitive title.   The badge certainly is related to the NSKOV, which was a Party-affiliated organization responsible for the organization and welfare of disabled war veterans and their relatives.   This author is unable to shed any further light on this badge other than to point out that a far greater number of badges existed than was previously believed, and that more information is still required.

Besides the basic diamond-shaped badge bearing the standard NSKOV insigne (Iron Cross on a sword surrounded by an elongated oakleaf wreath) on an enamel field, this badge existed with these variations (possible grades?):

a.   All white enamel field with a thin gold line to distinguish a white enamel edge.

b.   White enamel field with a thin gold line to distinguish a blue enamel edge.

Variation with Gold Oakleaf Border

c. Same as a. above, but with the addition of a gold oakleaf wreath.

d. Same as b. above, but with the addition of a gold oakleaf wreath.

The reverse was plain with a vertical needle clasp. Purpose, criteria and manner of wear of the award are not known.

POLICE ALPINE/HIGH ALPINE EXPERT BADGE
(Gendarmerie Alpine/Hochalpinistabzeichen)

The Police Expert Alpine and High Alpine badges were not awards, but were rather qualification badges awarded by the police organization to its members who qualified as expert mountaineers (Alpinist) or high mountaineers (Hochalpinist - qualified at the higher levels). Both badges were designed and produced by the L. Klein firm of Vienna, Austria. Both were probably introduced sometime in 1936. Allegedly only seven of the High Alpine badges were awarded, but no data can be found to confirm or deny this. This limited figure is questionable since both were qualification badges rather than awards. It is probable that there were three classes of each badge - bronze, silver and gold.

It is not known what the exact criteria for award were, but it can be assumed that they were related to various alpine skills such as climbing, rappeling, traversing, etc., with the High Alpinist badge being awarded for similar skills at high altitudes. Such skills were required in the mountains of Bavaria, and in the Tyrol once Austria was annexed.

R. McCarthy

Obverse   **Reverse**

Both badges measured approximately 63mm at their highest points, and 33mm wide. The High Alpinist badge design focused about the police emblem with a background of white enamel. This was surrounded by an oval edelweiss wreath of

Police officers celebrate the 1936 Reichsparteitag in a Nürnberg Gasthaus.

colored enamel. Surmounting the top of the wreath was a banner bearing the inscription 'Gendarmerie Hoch Alpinist' (Police High Alpinist), with a background of green enamel. Running lengthwise was a mountaineer's pick or stock. The Alpine badge was basically identical in design, but the wreath did not have the enamel work, and the banner read 'Gendarmerie Alpinist' (Police Alpinist).

POLICE EXPERT SKIER BADGE
(Polizei-Schiführerabzeichen)

Another of the police qualification badges was the Police Expert Skier Badge (Polizei-Schiführerabzeichen) which was introduced sometime in 1942. It was rendered to members of the police organization who successfully passed the Police Ski

Photos not to scale

Obverse   Reverse

Instructors Advanced Examination administered in the winter of 1941, or who had previously passed the expert skier course five times.

The badge was oval, measuring 44m high by 35mm wide, and was finished in dull aluminum paint with yellow background in the lettering and skis. It centered about the basic police emblem with a pair of skis running diagonally through the lower portion of the insigne. Surrounding the emblem was an oval field bearing the inscription 'Polizei Schi-Führer' (Police Expert Skier).

It was not an award, and so could only be worn on the winter sport uniform.

CIVIL PILOT

Pilots of the government-controlled civil airlines, or Lufthansa, and civilian pilots employed as instructors with the clandestine Luftwaffe were authorized to wear the Civil Pilot's badge. This badge was in no way an award, but was rather a qualification badge. To receive it the recipient had to be a licensed pilot, and employed either by the Lufthansa or the Luftwaffe.

The badge measured 81mm long, and took the form of blue enamel wings with gold feather lines projecting from a gold swastika. The reverse bore the manufacturer's logo (normally Juncker), and had a flat horizontal pin. The badge was worn above the left breast pocket.

The badge was bestowed in a dark blue hard case with the inscription 'Zivil-Flugzeugführer' (Civil Pilot) embossed in gold on the lid. The interior of the lid was dark blue satin, while the lower section was dark blue velvet.

Table Medals

The Reichsparteitag plaque 1939 was designed by Professor Richard Klein, and was produced in gold (1st Place), silver (2nd Place) and bronze (3rd Place). It was intended to be awarded for the competitions held during the week-long Party meeting held at Nürnberg. Due to the outbreak of the war, the rally never took place, and the plaques were never awarded.

NON-PORTABLE AWARDS

Awards of an official, semi-official and unofficial nature were often rendered in non-portable form.   As one would infer from the term, these awards were not intended to be worn, but displayed.   This type of award was normally presented in a presentation case, and unlike a portable award, was usually double-faced.   Because these awards were for display only, they were often referred to as 'table medals'.

National non-portable awards, which have been discussed previously, were accorded special recognition, whereas all other non-portable awards were rank-ordered below and enjoyed lesser degrees of recognition.   For example, the Plaque for the Donation of Horses was an officially instituted award given in the name of the Führer, but it was not accorded recognition as a national award.   Private, semi-private or unofficial non-portable awards received no recognition whatsoever beyond the immediate group or organization rendering them.

The non-portable award largely recognized service or achievement within a certain organization.   It was not uncommon for the purpose of the award to be struck or engraved into the reverse.   Whether or not an award document was rendered with the award largely depended on the organization making the presentation.

PLAQUE FOR DONATION OF HORSES, ETC.
(Plakette für Zurverfügungstellung von Pferden u.s.w.)

The Plaque for Donation of Horses, etc. (Plakette für Zurverfügungstellung von Pferden u.s.w.) was instituted by Hitler on 24 February 1937 to be presented to persons who donated horses, stables, parks and other material related to the advancement of horsemanship.

The obverse of the black iron plaque, which measured 137mm at its widest point, depicted a horse standing atop a national emblem.   An oakleaf wreath encircled the outer edge.   The reverse also had the oakleaf wreath at the outer edge, with the SA insigne at the base.   The inscription 'Für Verdienste um die Wehrhafte Ertüchtigung der Deutschen Reiterjugend" (For Service in the Pre-Military Training of Young German Riders), with a facsimile of Hitler's signature below, forms the central motif of the reverse.

Obverse to exact scale

The plaque, which was designed by Paul Casberg, was presented with an ornate award document signed by the head of the N. S. R. K., SA-Obergruppenführer Litzmann.

Reverse to exact scale

MEDALLION "FOR OUTSTANDING ACHIEVEMENTS IN THE TECHNICAL BRANCH OF THE AIR FORCE"
(Medaille "Für ausgezeichnete Leistungen im technischen Dienst der Luftwaffe")

The medallion for outstanding achievements in the technical branch of the Luftwaffe was instituted by Reichsmarschall Göring in July 1940 to be awarded to those persons who had made a significant contribution to the technical development of the Luftwaffe, but not to the point of qualifying for a higher distinction.

The round silver medallion measured 74mm, and was either silver or silver plate. Those that were produced from silver bore the silver content number on the

Obverse

Reverse

rim. Some examples finished in a dark burnished color are known to have been produced as well, but these specimens might simply reflect a fall-off in quality control.

The reverse of the medallion bore a profile of Göring and the inscription 'Der Oberbefehlshaber der Luftwaffe Reichsmarschall Göring' (The Commander-in-Chief of the Air Force, Reichsmarschall Göring). The obverse bore the national emblem of the Luftwaffe and the inscription 'Für ausgezeichnete Leistungen im technischen Dienst der Luftwaffe' (For Outstanding Achievements in the Technical Branch of the Air Force).

The medallion was presented in a black hard case without a lid designation. The interior of the lid was white satin, while the base was blue satin, and was compartmented to hold the award.

THE FÜHRER PLAQUE

The Führer Plaque was an officially recognized non-portable award. This was largely presented to middle-ranking political and state officials in recognition of special achievement.

The basic award measured 95mm wide by 141mm high. The bronze plaque featured a profile of Hitler in relief with a raised inscription below. As in the case of the piece illustrated, it was also possible for the person making the award to have a special inscription engraved on the obverse.   The reverse also bore a raised inscription stating that the award was presented in the name of the Führer, and giving the reason behind the award.   It was not uncommon for the portion of the reverse inscription that referred to the official nature of the award to be eliminated during casting.   It is assumed that this was done only to those awards that were, for some reason, not accorded official recognition.   An example of the removal of the last two

Obverse of the bronze Führer Plaque.   This example bears the addition of the special dedication by the person making the award.   Note the initials 'MH' under the profile.   It is assumed that these are the initials of the designer of the plaque.

ERSTE, VOM FÜHRER
UND DER REICHSLEITUNG
FÜR SEHR GUT BEFUNDENE,
NACH NATURSTUDIEN
GEARBEITETE PLAKETTE.
IM OFFIZIELLEN VERTRIEB
DER ZEUGMEISTEREIEN.

The reverse of the plaque has a raised inscription which, in this particular example, indicates the official nature of the award. Note the manufacturer's mark to the left of the profile. The manufacturer's mark can also be found at the top of the plaque.

Obverse Translation: "The supposition for action is the will and the courage for truth."
Reverse Translation: "The first plaque produced from a live sitting, which the Führer and Reichsleitung have found to be very good."

lines on the reverse inscription would be where a city might wish to award the plaque as an Honor Prize.

Unlike most non-portable awards, this particular award was constructed so that it might be hung on the wall.

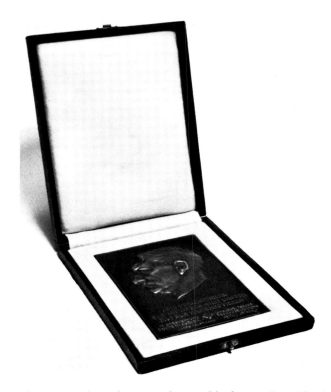

The presentation case for the award was black, and void of any outer markings. The plaque was recessed into the lower section of the case, which was finished in gray or silver-gray velvet. The lid was finished in gray or silver-gray satin, and sometimes bore the addition of a silk band with special designation pertaining to the award.

NSFK NATIONAL FLYING COMPETITION

Each year the NSFK sponsored the national flying competitions. Routes were designated, times recorded, and winning pilots recognized. In addition to the pilots who won the prizes, ground control personnel connected with the competitions were also recognized for special achievement by the presentation of a bronze plaque. The obverse of the oval plaque depicted the NSFK emblem and the inscription 'Nationalsozialistisches Fliegerkorps Deutschlandflug 1938'. The reverse bore a quotation, the signature in relief of the NSFK-Korpsführer, Christiansen, and a serial number.

The plaque was presented in a black case bearing no lid designation. The inside of the lid was white satin bearing the gold inscription 'Nationalsozialistisches Fliegerkorps Der Korpsführer'. The lower section was compartmented, and finished in dark blue velvet. Secured inside the lid was the award certificate.

Obverse

Reverse

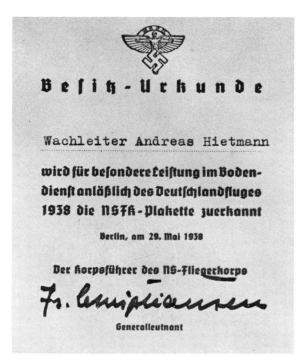

The award certificate indicates that the award is for special achievement for ground service in connection with the 1938 National Flying Competition. It is dated 29 May 1938, and signed by NSFK Korpsführer Christiansen.

SOARING COMPETITION PRIZE

Shown here is the prize awarded by NSFK Group 6 from Silesia to the winning glider pilot in the 1939 competition held at Grunau. The plaque is dull gray metal, with the reverse being completely void of markings. It was presented in a black case without

323

any lid designation.   The inside of the lid was white satin with the inscription 'NSFK. Gruppe 6 Schlesien' in gold.   The lower portion of the case was compartmented, and finished in blue velvet.   Secured inside the lid was the award certificate.

1934 COMMEMORATIVE PLAQUETTE FOR THE NÜRNBERG RALLY COMPETITIONS

A porcelain plaquette was presented by Nürnberg officials to commemorate the competitions held during the 1934 Nürnberg Rally.   The central motif was in gold, and depicted the national emblem (similar to that on the Blood Order) overlooking the Nürnberg Castle.   The outer circle was finished in a reddish-brown color, and bore the inscription 'Deutsche Kampfspiele Nürnberg 1934' (German Competition Games - Nürnberg 1934).   The outer rim was finished in gold.   The reverse bore the manufacturer's logo.

The plaquette was presented in a dark red case without exterior markings.   The inside of the lid was white satin, and bore the inscription 'Gegeben von der Stadt Nürnberg' (Presented by the City of Nürnberg) in red letters.   The lower section was compartmented, and finished in white velvet.   What the exact criteria for award were

is not known.

Cased Commemorative Plaquette for the Nürnberg Rally Competitions. (Not to scale)

SERVICE MEDAL OF THE BAVARIAN INDUSTRIAL LEAGUE
(Verdienstmedaille des Bayerischen Industriellen Verbandes)

A commemorative medallion was awarded by the Industrial League of Bavaria to honor long and loyal service to industry. The awards were rendered in gold, silver and probably bronze as well, depending on the length of service. This award is not be be confused with the long service awards struck and issued by the State of Bavaria

Oddera

Obverse

Reverse

Note the designer's logo and silver content on the rim of the Service Medal.

Oddera

The lid of the burgundy colored case bore the gold dedication 'Service Medal of the Bavarian Industrial League'. The interior of the lid bears the jeweller's logo on white satin, while the medallion is set in blue velvet.

in recognition of loyal service to industry as the medallion was presented by the Bavarian Industrial League, and not by the State Government of Bavaria.

The round medallion measured 50mm in diameter, and was the design of Carl Pollath. The obverse depicts a laborer receiving laurels from a woman. At the base of the medallion is the inscription 'Ehre der Arbeit' (Honor to Labor). There have been examples noted that have had the national emblem affixed to this lower area over the inscription. The reverse has a laurel wreath surrounding a beehive and three 'busy' bees. Below the beehive is the inscription 'Für langjährige treue Dienst vom Bayerischen Industriellen Verband' (For Longstanding Loyal Service From the Bavarian Industrial League). The silver content number was usually stamped into the rim following the jeweller's mark.

The medallion was presented in a burgundy colored hard case, probably in conjunction with an award certificate.

COMMEMORATIVE RELIEF OF THE CENTRAL GROUP OF THE RAILWAY ATHLETIC AND SPORT ASSOCIATION
(Erinnerungsrelief der Zentralstelle der Reichsbahn-Turn-und Sportvereine)

A special 10-year commemorative non-portable award was instituted by the National Railway Athletic and Sport Association in 1937. It was given to 500 of its

200,000 members in recognition of special achievement, especially in connection with the 1936 Olympics where seven of its members had participated, and two had become recipients of the Olympic Medal.

The bas-relief depicted male and female sports enthusiasts along with persons representing several occupations within the National Railway Service. The dates at the base of the award, 1926-1936, represent the ten-year anniversary of the association. The center motif bore the national eagle with the athletic association swastika on its chest.

The 108mm award was designed by Kunze-Richter.

AUTOBAHN COMMEMORATIVE PLAQUETTE

A plaquette was ceremoniously embedded in a stone to commemorate the construction of each 1,000 kilometers of the Autobahn, the major interstate road system connecting all the regions of Germany. In addition, selected persons connected with the building were awarded an identical plaquette, and all persons connected with the construction were given a miniature pin of identical design. The design for each 1,000 kilometers of the Autobahn completed differed. Shown here is the plaquette for the 2,000 kilometer mark. The reverse is plain.

Autobahn Commemorative Plaquette

MISCELLANEOUS SPORTS MEDALLIONS

The winning prize for the SA Sport Competition held by SA Group Bayer. Ostmark in 1939 was a double faced porcelain plaquette. The obverse of the white porcelain award bore the SA Sport badge, the SA emblem and the dedication of the award. The outer rim was finished in gold. The reverse had an oakleaf wreath with gold highlights and the inscription 'Dem 1. Sieger' (To the 1st Place Winner) in raised gold lettering.

The award was presented in a black case without lid markings. The inside of the lid was white satin, while the lower compartmented section was dark blue velvet raised to a plateau.

Obverse

Reverse

Tom Jones

NSFK medallion for Five Years Honorable Service Achievement.   The medallion is serial numbered 711, and presented in the name of the NSFK Korpsführer, Generaloberst Keller.   The finish is oxidized silver.

Golden SA Honor Prize of SA Group Niederrhein competitive games 16-18 June 1939. The medallion was presented in a black hard case with a mouse-gray lower base interior. There is no lid designation.

MILITARY NON-PORTABLE AWARDS

Unofficial awards were presented by military units for special achievement or recognition. These awards were usually privately purchased from a shop specializing in trophies, mementos, etc., and were presented at all levels. The silver medallion bore different military scenes so that one might be selected to suit a particular occasion. For example, a tank battalion wishing to bestow an award might select a medallion bearing a tank (see example), while an Infantry unit might select one bearing the head of a helmeted soldier.

The 40mm medallion had a large area on the reverse to allow for a special dedication or presentation inscription to be engraved. At the top reverse of the medallion was a sprig of oakleaves.

The medallion came in a gray cardboard box with a gray velvet compartmented base that was capable of being propped up for display.

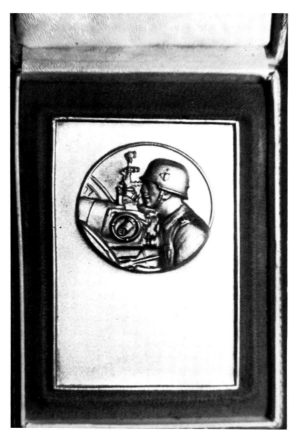

Another example of an unofficial military award. The rectangular award is silver, and depicts a gunner sighting an artillery piece. It was probably intended as a gunnery award, with the details of the award to be engraved in the plain area below the bas-relief. The reverse is plain. The presentation box is cardboard, and finished in a blue-gray color. The lower interior is compartmented, and finished in gray velvet.

This young woman is shown wearing the War Volunteer Service Badge of the RADwJ.

𝕸𝖎𝖘𝖈𝖊𝖑𝖑𝖆𝖓𝖊𝖔𝖚𝖘

AWARDS OF THE GERMAN SHOOTING LEAGUE
(Deutscher Schützen-Verband Abzeichen)

German shooting clubs had been established long before Adolf Hitler took an interest in them. Still, he viewed the clubs as having great potential, possibly serving to further the Nazi movement, enlist new members, expand the areas controlled by the Nazi Party, and to prepare Germany's youth for a seemingly inevitable clash of arms. It was recognized that, through increased emphasis, marksmanship could be advanced in a wider spectrum of the civilian population.

While the primary purpose of the shooting clubs, now gathered together under the control of the German Shooting League (Deutscher Schützen-Verband), was to form a competitive outlet for shooting enthusiasts, they also served to form a social alliance among shooters. Shooting contests were gala events at all levels of competition. Competitors took their shooting very seriously as the honor of their team, their village, their state or possibly their country was at stake. After the competition, the beer flowed freely, and an opportunity was provided for the competitors to display the awards that they had won.

Uniforms were normally worn during shooting events, and on the uniforms were the many medals and neck awards that had previously been won. The sponsor of the competitions, the German Shooting League, had the responsibility for establishing and rendering these awards, which had no fixed pattern, and like Rally badges, were often designed for a single event or competition.

Like all organizations in Germany after 1934, the German Shooting League fell under the control of the Nazi Party, and was subjected to restrictions imposed by the various governmental agencies. This was especially true of the many awards which had been created for the League competitors. Due to the unofficial nature of these awards, the Minister of the Interior established regulations strictly governing their wear, to the extent that they could be worn only on the shooting uniform when en route to and from, and while at, events held by the League. Wearing this type of award was strictly prohibited while in civilian clothes.

The awards that follow are but a small sampling of the many awards created by the German Shooting League.

| Obverse | Reverse |

Participant medal in bronze given to the entrants in final shooting competition sponsored by the Railway and Post Office Athletic League of Stuttgart, 1935. Such competitions were held largely to raise money to support the League's annual expenditures.

| Obverse | Reverse |

3rd Place shooting medal awarded for the standing position competition held at Steinkirchen in 1937. The medal is silver with a silver and black enamel circular emblem of the Shooting League. The suspension ribbon is green and white, the traditional colors of the Shooting League.

Obverse

Reverse

Entrants medal given to all participants who shot in the Winter Relief fund raising competition held on 24 March 1938. The medal is gold with a green and white suspension bow-ribbon. This medal is quite indicative of the efforts to combine sports, fund raising and propaganda in the awards and tokens of the period.

Obverse

Reverse

Bronze participant's medal given to entrants of the shooting competition held in 1939. Considering the nature of the competition and dates stamped into the medal, and the frontal motif combining Hitler and von Hindenburg, it is possible that the basic medal may have been left over from earlier period stocks.

SINGING COMPETITION AWARDS

State and national singing competitions in Germany remain a carry-over from medieval times. Singing provided a social outlet for the hard-working farmers and laborers alike. The individual and group singers represented their villages in the spirit of friendly competition. The singing competitions that were held each year provided various awards to be won, but more important was the recognition that a winner earned for his village or state.

It would appear that the awards were rendered in bronze (third), silver (second) and gold (first place), and took the form of medals, badges and medallions.

Shown here are two such awards given for excellence in singing.

Obverse

Reverse

Bronze medal measuring 50mm awarded for the competition held in Saarbrücken in 1936.

This appears to be more of a commemorative medal presented for loyal service in the furtherance of singing rather than a competitive medal. The reverse of the gold lapel medal is engraved 'Sänger Gauführer Dr. M. Schwarz 1936', and is marked 800.

Award in its presentation case. The case is finished in a burgundy color, and is void of any exterior markings. The inside lid bears the manufacturer's logo, and the paper attached to the lower blue velvet section is the tab of the distributor.

WEHRSPORT DEVICE

The Wehrsport device, worn on both collars by select members of the right-wing Steel Helmet organization (Stahlhelm), was not an award, nor was it the forerunner of the SA Wehrabzeichen. It was intended as a recognition device only. It is shown here simply for clarification. It should be noted that the Steel Helmet organization already had an existing award which served as a sports award - the Wehrsportkreuz.

Example shown is not to scale. **The measurement from tip of right acorn to left tip of oak leaf is 57mm.**

SUBMARINE SHIPYARD WORKERS BADGE

Except for a single article in the <u>Grüne Presse</u> (<u>Green Press</u>) dated 27 August 1944, little information is available concerning an award presented to builders of submarines. The article makes specific reference to an award of the Shipyard Workers Badge (Werftarbeiter Abzeichen) being presented to submarine construction workers.

The article, which was accompanied by a photo, describes the badge as having a submarine passing through a gear bearing the national emblem at the top. No other information has been found that would provide data pertaining to the size, criteria for award or manner of wear. However, it is strongly believed that the award takes the form of a lapel pin rather than a pin-back badge.

339

SERVICE AND RANK INSIGNIA OF THE RADwJ

The insignia discussed in this section are not classified as awards or decorations in the true sense of this work. They are service or rank insignia found only in the female branch of the National Labor Service (Reichsarbeitsdienst der weiblichen Jugend - RADwJ). These insignia are included because they are often seen in photographs, and could easily be mistaken for awards.

Egon Jantke was the principal designer for the RAD, having entered into their employ in 1936. He was responsible for the design of the RAD hewer, the RAD service medals, and most of the service and rank insignia which follow.

The leadership branch of the RADwJ was divided into two sections; the first section was basically made up of aspiring leaders, aged 18 to 21, who underwent a series of service tests before they could advance in rank. They started out as 'Labor Maidens' (Arbeitsmädel), and upon completion of tests for that position, were awarded badges of rank to denote their positions. The progressive rank structure became rather complex where the rank badges were concerned. Three basic rank badges existed - each of which measured slightly larger than the next lower grade. They were all round, and were worn as a brooch at the throat. Each incorporated the basic insigne of the RADwJ - the swastika between two ears of barley. Four rank distinctions existed - iron, bronze, silver and gold, with grade distinctions within each rank. The grade and rank breakdown was as follows:

IRON: Arbeitsmaid (badge A); Kameradschaftsälteste (badge B):

BRONZE: Jungführerin (A); Maidenunterführerin (B); Maidenführerin (C)

SILVER: Maidenoberführerin (B); Maidenhauptführerin (C)

GOLD: Stabsführerin (A); Stabsoberführerin (B); Stabshauptführerin (C)

Badge A

Badge B

Badge C

The second grouping of female leaders were those between the ages of 21 and 35 who had passed their tests, and who were promoted largely on the basis of merit. It was this group that held the higher leadership positions. This group was also entitled to wear badges of rank in brooch form at the throat, but the exact rank breakdown is not known. The badge was oval in shape, measuring 46mm wide by 35mm high. It bore the RADwJ insigne as the central motif surrounded by twisted rope. The rank badge for this group was finished in bronze, silver and gold.

Members of the RADwJ were eligible for yet another award worn in the form of a round brooch. This measured 44mm, and bore the inscription "Work for our people - work for ourselves - German Women's Labor Service" around the outer edge. In the center was the swastika in the middle of some barley ears; this was not the same as the standard RADwJ emblem. It is presumed that this was an award in recognition of special achievement or service in the RAD, but the specific criteria for award are not known. Criteria for award must have been rather rigid as each award is serial numbered on the reverse.

The younger members of the RADwJ could also qualify for service achievement badges. In September 1941 the RAD established the Volunteer Labor Service to support the war effort. A special badge was instituted to recognize services rendered by the young women who participated in this program. The badge was in brooch form and consisted of a swastika between two barley ears with a banner bearing the initials 'RADwJ'. The War Volunteer Service badge (Kriegshilfsdienst-Abzeichen) could be earned after one month of service in support of the war effort (work in a hospital, factory, railway function, etc.), and was worn on the left breast. The brooch was finished in old silver.

**War Volunteer Service
Badge of the RADwJ**

Hoover Institution

Those girls in the RADwJ who did not hold leadership positions, and who had completed one year of service, were authorized to wear the membership badge of the RADwJ. The round brooch measured 44mm, and was finished in a gray color. It was worn at the throat.

Membership Badge of the RADwJ

UNATTRIBUTED

After many years of research this particular medal still remains unattributed. This silver medal measures 33mm, and is suspended from a cornflower blue ribbon. The obverse bears the Prussian eagle with a swastika on its chest. The outer edge of the medal has laurel leaves running to the left and oakleaves running to the right. The reverse is void of any design.

It is assumed that this piece was intended for award in recognition of a particular event or service since space on the back was provided for an appropriate dedication to be engraved.

No other information is currently available.

Obverse	Reverse

This bronze medal appears to be an organizational medal, but no other information is available. The reverse shows what appears to be a soldier behind a frontier fortification protecting a woman and her child (symbol of the nation?). The title indicates 'Zone Offenburg Lines 1938'. The obverse depicts a man digging over a symbol of the organization 'GB - Grün u. Bilfingera'.

The laborers of this Cologne-based firm who participated in the construction of the Siegfried Line, were allegedly given this medal.

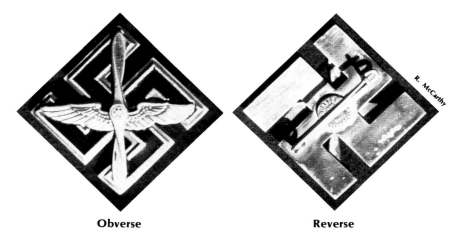

Obverse   Reverse

Unattributed badge. A black enamel swastika with silver border with silver winged propeller affixed.   The reverse bears the manufacturer's logo.

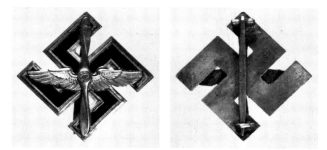

This variant of the above badge was produced by a different manufacturer, and has a serial number on the pin bar.

Novelty medal of unknown history.   In the center are the profiles of Hindenburg and Hitler finished in gold.   The arms of the cross are silver, while the oakleaves between the arms are gold. On the reverse of the gold eagle that surmounts the cross is a fixed loop for the suspension ribbon.   No further data is available.

345

Addendum to Vol. 1

Pg. 18:

George Robinson

Schlageter Bund Commemorative badge marking the tenth anniversary of the death of Albert Leo Schlageter at the hands of the French. This specimen was presented to Viktor Lutze, and is serial numbered '7'. The smaller badge is a lapel pin. Note the spelling of 'Victor', a common error even to the Germans.

Pg. 40: Solid bronze versions have been encountered bearing the manufacturer's logo.

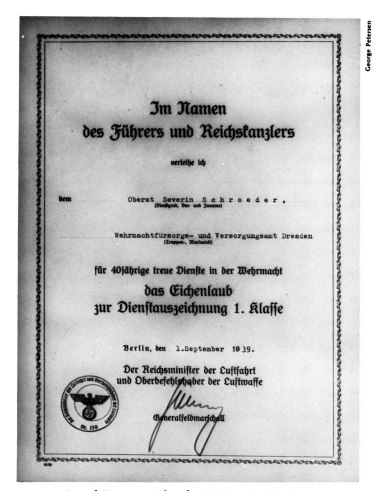

Im Namen
des Führers und Reichskanzlers

verleihe ich

dem   Oberst Severin S c h r o e d e r ,
               (Dienstgrad, Vor- und Zuname)

       Wehrmachtfürsorge- und Versorgungsamt Dresden
                (Truppen-, Marineteil)

für 40jährige treue Dienste in der Wehrmacht

das Eichenlaub
zur Dienstauszeichnung 1. Klasse

Berlin, den   1.September 19 39.

Der Reichsminister der Luftfahrt
und Oberbefehlshaber der Luftwaffe

Generalfeldmarschall

Nr. 150

Award Document for the 40-Year Service Cross.

Pg. 55:   The second pattern medal was designed by Professor Puchinger of Vienna, who also designed the 1938 'Anschluss' stamp which commemorated the union of Austria with Germany. An order dated 14 June 1938 and signed by Martin Bormann stated the following prerequisites for Austrians to get the medal. All recipients had to be National Socialists,

a. who as a member of the NSDAP took an active part in the struggle for unification.

b. who were injured during the struggle for unification, were imprisoned, or because of active participation in the movement lost their Austrian citizenship.

c. who were murdered or executed while fighting for the movement. (In this case the medal was awarded to the victim's parents or widow.)

NOTE
Application for the medal had to be made before
10 April 1938.

Pg. 72:

Detailed photos of the Commemorative Medal for the Campaign of 1939/1940. The ribbon colors are black/red/black/white/red/white/black/red/black.

Pg. 74:   Change 384th Infantry Division to read 44th Infantry Division.

Pg. 89:

Otto Quenstedt

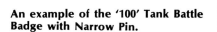

An example of the '100' Tank Battle Badge with Narrow Pin.

348

D. Frailey

U-Boat Badge with Diamonds
This U-Boat Badge with Diamonds was awarded to Kapitänleutnant Georg Lassen, commander of U 160, and seventh highest scoring U-Boat commander in World War II. The badge was manufactured by the firm of Schwerin in Berlin and is made out of gilded silver with a swastika with nine diamonds separately affixed to the badge. The recipient of the U-Boat Badge with Diamonds had to be a holder of the Oak Leaves of the Knight's Cross. The award was personally handed to Lassen by Grossadmiral Raeder in 1943 and there was no case or document accompanying the badge.

Pg. 122: Since the Submarine War Badge with Diamonds was produced only by C. Schwerin of Berlin, and was awarded without a case, the recipient could have used any firm's case for protection (i.e., the Godet firm of Berlin). 349

D. Frailey

BESITZZEUGNIS

Im Namen
des Oberbefehlshabers
der Kriegsmarine
verleihe ich
dem
Oberfunkmaaten
Fritz Gentes
N 135437
das
Kriegsabzeichen für Hilfskreuzer

An Bord, den *1. Dez. 1941*

(Dienstsiegel)

Eyssen
Konteradmiral
und Kommandant
(Dienstgrad, Dienststellung)

This Auxiliary Cruiser Badge document is for Ship 45 (<u>Komet</u>) and is signed by Konteradmiral Eyssen, the commander.

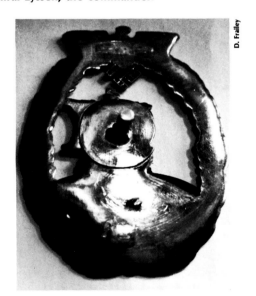

D. Frailey

This Auxilliary Cruiser War Badge with Diamonds was awarded to Kapitän zur S Bernhard Rogge. The badge is gilded silver with a silver-grey globe and has 15 d monds set into the swastika. Kapitän Rogge's badge originally had a vertical p mounting but because the catch often opened on his uniform, he had a jewe remove the pin and add a screwback mounting. Kapitän Rogge received his bad with diamonds personally from Grossadmiral Raeder after having been awarded t Oak Leaves to the Knight's Cross as commander of the Raider <u>Atlantis</u>. The awa was presented without a document.

Pg. 139:   Delete Swords and Diamonds from line 7.

The firm of Adolf Bock designed the High Seas Fleet War Badge.   Bock was an official artist (painter) of the German Navy during WWI and WWII.   Herr Bock stated that he also submitted a design for the Auxiliary Cruiser War Badge, but without the lower rigging.   He was informed that the design should feature the lower rigging.   He refused to include it in his design, so the contract was awarded to the Peekhaus Firm.

Im Namen des Oberbefehlshabers der Kriegsmarine

verleihe ich dem

Leutnant (Ing.)

Paul W e i d l i c h

für die Teilnahme an den Kriegsfahrten des

Schlachtschiff „Scharnhorst"

das

Flotten=Kriegsabzeichen

Den 13. März 1942.

Der Befehlshaber der Schlachtschiffe

In Vertretung!

Kapitän zur See

Award Document for the High Seas Fleet War Badge.   Note that it lists the recipient's ship,   the <u>Scharnhorst</u>.

Pg. 143:

A photo of a 1st pattern E-Boat Badge reverse with the more common horizontal pin arrangement.   Note the manufacturer's logo.

Pg. 151:

BESITZZEUGNIS

Auf Grund der Ermächtigung des Oberbefehlshabers
der Kriegsmarine verleihe ich dem

das

Kriegsabzeichen

für die

Marineartillerie

Cuxhaven, den 6.   194

Vizeadmiral
und Küstenbefehlshaber Deutsche Bucht

A variation award document for the War Badge for Coastal Artillery.

Pg. 154:

U. 1
                                                          den 9.5.1945.

        Kommando HKS "Kamerun"

        Der Führer der Unterseeboote Nordmeer hat dem Oblt. (Ing)
.W e i d l i c h , Paul vom Kommando HKS "Kamerun" heute die
U - Bootsfrontspange in Silber verliehen.

                                        Fregattenkapitän und
                                Führer der Unterseeboote Nordmeer

An Award Document for the U-Boat Close Combat Clasp in silver, dated one day after the war ended.

Pg. 155:

Award Document for the Marinefrontspange in Bronze.

353

This Marinefrontspange in Bronze and the Urkunde were obtained from Martin Schmitz, who received the award as a Stabsoberfeuerwerker in the Kriegsmarine. The badge was manufactured on board the Führerschiffe <u>Reiher</u> and awarded to members of the 10th Sicherungsdivision who filled the requirement of having layed 275 mines. The Urkunde is signed by Fregattenkapitän Hugo Heydel.

The award was given on 14 May 1945, five days after the war was officially over. The 10th Sicherungsdivision operated, however, in the Kurland area until 21 May 1945 bringing refugees to Germany from Soviet held territory.

Pg. 157: Grades V-VII (Clasps) also exist in embroidered cloth.

Pg. 164: While the last officially recorded date for the award of the Pilot's badge was 2 May 1944, the award document presented to Unteroffizier Eckhard Willige along with his Pilot's badge was dated 26 March 1945.

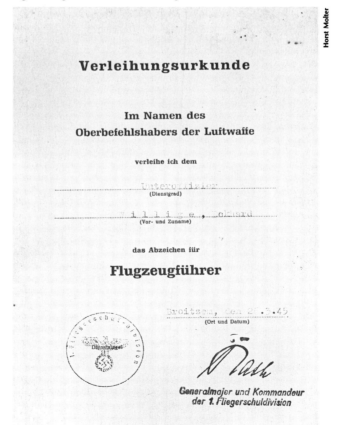

VERLEIHUNGS-URKUNDE

ICH VERLEIHE
SEINER EXCELLENZ
DEM HERRN
CAVALIERE

BENITO MUSSOLINI

CHEF DER KÖNIGLICHEN UND
KAISERLICHEN REGIERUNG
ROM
DAS GOLDENE
FLUGZEUGFÜHRER-UND
BEOBACHTER-ABZEICHEN

BERLIN/APRIL 1937

DER REICHSMINISTER DER LUFTFAHRT
UND OBERBEFEHLSHABER DER LUFTWAFFE

Göring.

GENERALOBERST

Award Document for the Pilot/Observer Badge with Diamonds presented to Benito Mussolini.

Pg. 174:   Minor variations of the Combined Pilot's and Observer's Badge in Gold
with Diamonds appear to exist.   One specimen is noted to have a total of
approximately 171 diamonds (estimated total weight 3.60 ct.).   It is constructed of 18kt yellow gold and platinum in a setting measuring 65mm
wide by 52mm high with a total weight of 41.5gm.

Pg. 190:

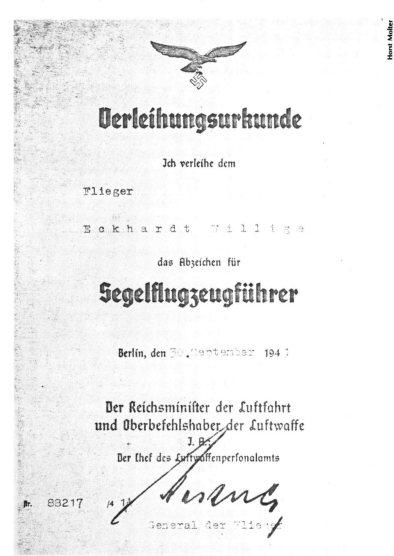

Award Document for the Glider Pilot's Badge.

Pg. 250:   It is interesting to note that the award document was presented on 1 March
1943 when Rommel bore the rank of Generalfeldmarschall. Yet the document bears the rank of Generaloberst.   It is apparent that pre-printed
stocks were used until exhausted.

Pg. 251:

A mountain troop patrol makes its way to the top of an Alpine slope during the closing days of the war.   The NCO leading the patrol wears the badge of a qualified mountain guide or Bergführer.   Just above this metal and enamel badge is a smaller badge which appears to be for first aid.

Pg. 259:

Award Document for the Black Wound Badge, presented to an Eastern Volunteer.

Pg. 266: For SS-Hauptsturmführer Karl Günsche read Otto Günsche. Walter Hewel was Foreign Minister von Ribbentrop's personal representative at FHQ.

Pg. 282:

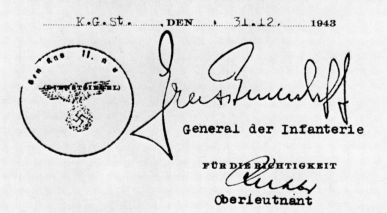

BESITZZEUGNIS

IM NAMEN DES FÜHRERS

WURDE DEM

Obergefreiten Karl Hafemeier

12./Gren. Rgt. 501

DER

DEMJANSK-SCHILD

VERLIEHEN

K.G.St. , DEN 31.12. 1943

General der Infanterie

FÜR DIE RICHTIGKEIT

Oberleutnant

Temporary Award Document for the Demjansk Shield presented by the Commander of Army Group North, General der Infanterie Graf Brockdorff-Ahlefeldt.

Preliminary Award Document for the Kuban Shield.

Besitzzeugnis

Im Namen

des Führers

wurde dem .... Korvettenkapitän
(Dienstgrad)

Hermann B ü c h t i n g
(Vor- und Familienname)

1.Schnellbootsflottille
(Truppenteil)

der **Kubanschild** verliehen.

H.Qu., den 8. Dezember 1944

Generalfeldmarschall

D. Frailey

Im Namen
und im Auftrag des Oberbefehlshabers der 20. Geb.Armee
Gen. d. Geb.Truppe Böhme-
wurde dem

Obergefreiten M e y e r , Karl

5./Geb.Jäg.Rgt. 143

der

Lapplandschild

verliehen.

O.U., 20. Juli 1945.

Obstlt. u. Rgt.Kdr.

Tom Jayne

Award Document for the Lapland Shield.

Pg. 285: A specimen of the Lapland Shield has been obtained which has black wool backing, reinforced by heavy paper, rather than a metal back-plate.

Pg. 323: Change genuine silver (line 9) to read silver plate.

Pg. 329: There exists an original specimen having five rivets - four with the same placement as the standard German manufacture, and the fifth rivet through the center of the badge.

Pg. 331:   The line that borders the outer side of the lid should correspond with the color of the German Cross (i.e., gold and silver).

Pg. 332:   Additional photographs of the German Cross in Gold with Diamonds are provided for the reader's interest.

German Cross in Gold with Diamonds
The gold wreath contains small diamonds throughout except on the date bar. The reverse shows a six rivet construction and the inscription 'Rath München' depicting the manufacturer of this particular specimen (and probably the others as well).

Pg. 337: The Iron Cross was also awarded in some cases for 'meritorious assistance of a senior commander', which allowed staff officers contributing to the success of a combat operation to receive the award as well.

Pg. 341:

E. Anderson

1939 Clasp to the 1914 Iron Cross IInd Class and its Issue Envelope.

Pg. 360: **Preliminary Award Document for the Oakleaves to the Knight's Cross of ▶ the Iron Cross.**

Pg. 372: A photo of the reverse of the Star of the Grand Cross is provided for the reader's interest. Note the four rivet construction. The red leather case ▶ bears an Iron Cross 1st Class on the center of the lid.

DER FÜHRER
UND OBERSTE BEFEHLSHABER
DER WEHRMACHT

HAT DEM

Kapitänleutnant

Georg L a s s e n

DAS EICHENLAUB
ZUM RITTERKREUZ DES
EISERNEN KREUZES

AM   7. März 1943   VERLIEHEN.

BERLIN, DEN   26. März 1943.

Fregattenkapitän
(Dienstgrad und Dienststellung)

Pg. 383: The Luftwaffe officer is in fact wearing the Order of the Crown of King Zvonimir, 1st Class, and not the Order of the Iron Trefoil.

Pg. 403: Mussert Cross: A specimen has been encountered that has no swords. It is a logical assumption that any award having swords would also have a corresponding grade without swords. The reverse of the specimen without swords has the wording as shown, but smaller in size.

Pg. 410: The series of variant ribbons for the 'Eastern Peoples' award IInd Class was originally obtained by the United States Government at the end of the war. Mr. Charles Stulga has provided me with another set of these awards so that exact information might be passed on to the reader. The ribbon in each case measures 26mm with a 2mm line down the center. The color variations by grade are as follows:

    Bronze: Lime green with light blue center stripe
    Silver: Dark green with dark blue center stripe
    Gold: Off white with dark red center stripe.

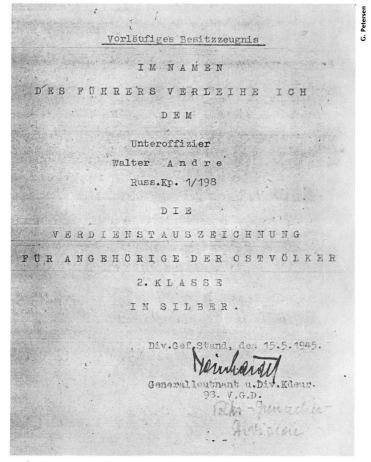

G. Petersen

Preliminary Award Document for 'Eastern People's' decoration, dated 15 May 1945.

Pg. 417:

Ron Weinand

Commemorative Medal for the Spanish Volunteers (Spanish Version)

A variation of the Spanish Medal is shown for the reader's interest. Unlike the standard pattern shown in Vol. 1, which is a one-piece stamping, this example is constructed in three pieces. The detail of this is more distinct, and differs slightly from the standard production piece. This specimen measures 37mm wide by 51mm high (including suspension loop at top of crown). The presentation case is red simulated leather with white satin interior lid and blue satin interior base. The case measures 117mm x 56mm x 22mm, and is fastened by means of a spring-tension release. There are no identification marks on either the medal or case.

Pg. 422:

E. Anderson

Illustrated is an excellent example of military miniatures which were worn on civilian clothes.

𝕬𝖉𝖉𝖊𝖓𝖉𝖚𝖒

Page:

8. Add to individual credits:
   Brock Clark
   Earl Grohs
   Gary Goetz
   Joseph Roth
   Roy Sather

12.

This elderly parent wears the Cross of Honor for Widows or Parents.

Cross of Honor for Non-Combatants.

Cross of Honor for Widows or Parents. At left is the standard pattern as worn suspended from the ribbon, while at right is a rare pinback version (specimens to scale).

20.

Cased German Olympic Games Decoration 2nd Class.

Size comparison of the three different presentation cases.

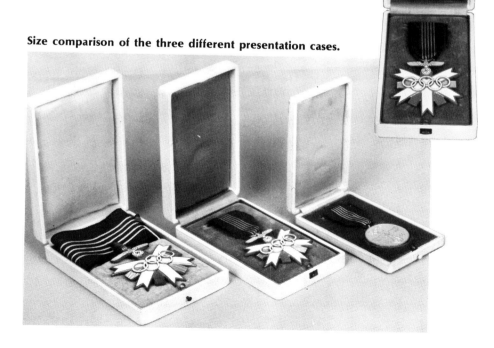

27.

Obverse and reverse photos of the Breast Star of the German National Prize for Art and Science.

28. End of sentence, line 7: "Each piece was marked by the jeweler with a personal code, and a dot-code was used for the correct assembly."

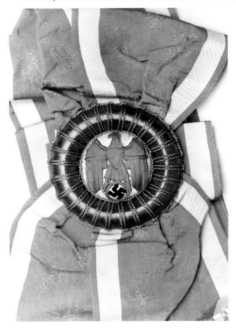

Detailed photographs of the rosette on the shoulder sash.

Presentation case for the Arts and Science Award. The sash was stored in the lower compartment, while the breast star was positioned on a tray inserted over the sash.

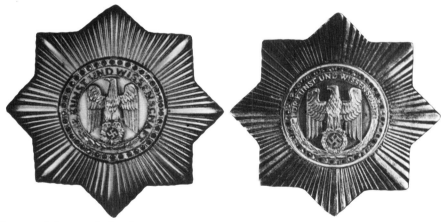

Two prototypes of the breast star are illustrated above. They were designed by Professor Herbert Zeitner.

It would appear that a few prototype designs were produced of this award, the design creation of Professor Herbert Zeitner. Additionally, existing specimens shown here would also indicate that a progressive series may have, in fact, been intended consisting of a neck order and a sash order. Each badge was assembled from over 20 different pieces, and was capable of being partially disassembled by means of an intricate bayonet-screw system. The neck order is finished in gold, while the sash order is finished partially in silver. The reverse of both pieces is identical in design. Speculation is that these were intended to designate position (i.e., neck order for the President of the Order, and the sash order for the Secretary of the Order) rather than part of the sequence of award.

Size comparison between the breast star (center), the sash order (left) and the neck order (right).

Sash Order

Neck Order

38.

1937 Series

Henry Ford is bestowed with the Grand Cross of the Order of the German Eagle by the German Consul in Cleveland, Karl Kapp, and the Consul from Detroit, Fritz Hailer. Date of award was July 1938. Note the six-pointed breast star.

Sash badge of the 1937 Grand Cross (1st pattern without fan).

Grand Cross of the Order of the German Eagle in Gold presented to German Foreign Minister, Joachim von Ribbentrop.

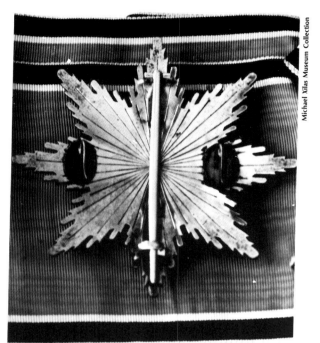

40. 1939 top block: add to text "Deutsche Verdienstmedaille mit Schwertern" on both case and wrapper.

42. Block 7 at bottom of page, 2nd line: "Eight-pointed silver star . . ." to read "Briefly six-pointed, but then eight-pointed . . ."

50.

Supporting tray for the sash badge and breast star (without swords) for the 1943 Ist Class.

53.

1937 Series

Service Cross 1st Class (without fan).

Early pattern (without fan) sash badge modified with
addition of the swords as introduced in 1939.

55.

2nd Class decoration with
the addition of swords.

56.

5th Class miniature.

57.

Note variation of eagle pattern on lid.

Paper wrapper for the Service Medal with Swords. Note the addition of the ink stamp designating "Bronze" award.

64.

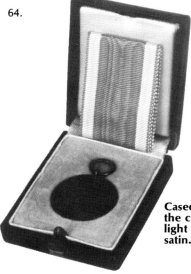

Cased Life Saving Medal with Ribbon. The exterior of the case is black simulated leather. The interior base is light blue velvet, while the interior of the lid is white satin.

65. Add after line 5: "The rim can be marked with the silver content and mint mark, e.g., "835 PR. M. BER." Additionally, one specimen mounted on a medal bar has been modified with a ribbon rosette about the outer perimeter to bring the small medal into comparative size with others."

68. Add at end of paragraph: "Miniatures were also produced for the early pattern Mother's Cross. It should be noted that specimens were also produced without any inscription for which there is no known reason. Miniatures without the inscription were also produced."

Full size and miniature Mother's Crosses fitted with pin-backs to allow them to be worn as brooches. Both are 2nd Pattern, with the full size in gold, and the miniature in silver.

69. End of line 5: "It would appear that the presentation case for the early pattern cross was with a black rather than dark blue cover."

79.

Variation pattern presentation case for the Honor Award. The configuration varies slightly, and the lid interior is white--otherwise the cases are the same. This specimen was awarded to Viktor Lutze.

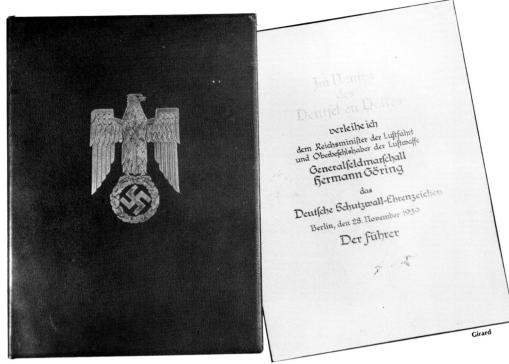

Award document and binder for the West Wall Medal presented to Göring.

83. Eagle Shield series.

The Eagle Shield of Germany award is of two-piece construction as shown above.

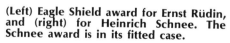

(Left) Eagle Shield award for Ernst Rüdin, and (right) for Heinrich Schnee. The Schnee award is in its fitted case.

HEINRICH
SCHNEE
DEM DEUTSCHEN
KOLONIAL-
PIONIER

DER FÜHRER
4.II.1941

85.

Exterior lid of the presentation case for the Goethe Medal for Art and Science depicts a gold national emblem and a gold perimeter border stamped on a dark blue simulated leather.

Charita

Goebbels presents the documentation for the Goethe Medal to recipient Paul Lincke. In the center is the Ober-burgermeister of Berlin holding the cased medal and the award document.

96. End of second paragraph: "It should be noted that badges for Kreissieger and Gausieger have been encountered bearing dates as early as 1935!"

104. Line 6: Not all cases bore the cog-wheel imprint as shown below, but rather had no exterior designation. One series in the author's collection is distinguished by the case color--black for iron, blue for silver, and red for gold. The interior lid of each is designated in gold "Dr.-Fritz-Todt-Preis"

105. Line 6: "Only found in stickpin form . . ." to read "Found in both stickpin and pinback form . . ."

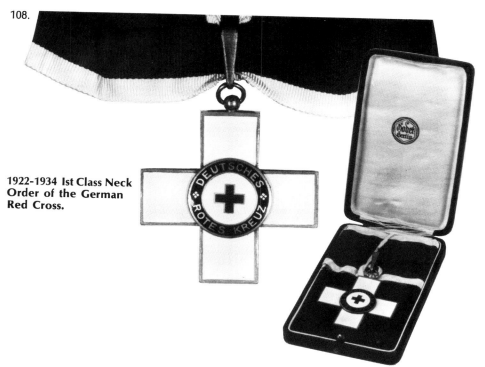

108.

1922-1934 Ist Class Neck Order of the German Red Cross.

As above, with presentation case.

Red Cross Breast Star, 1922-1934: The silver four-pointed star measures 80mm, and the enamel cross 40mm.

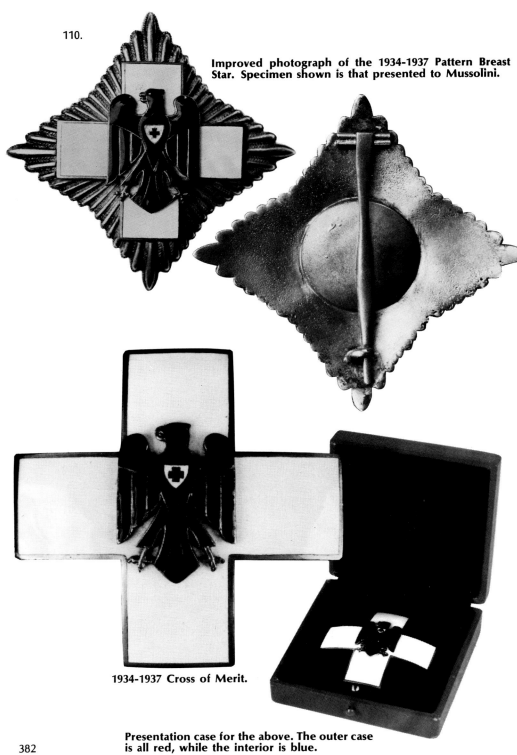

110.

Improved photograph of the 1934-1937 Pattern Breast Star. Specimen shown is that presented to Mussolini.

1934-1937 Cross of Merit.

Presentation case for the above. The outer case is all red, while the interior is blue.

382

113

1934-1937 Decoration of the Red Cross. The reverse is plain gold colored.

Cased version of the Ladies' Cross, which is identical to the above, but suspended from a bow rather than a straight ribbon. The case is red, and the interior blue.

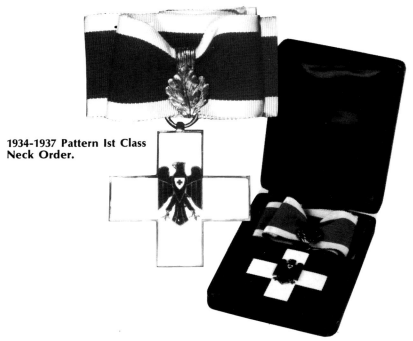

1934-1937 Pattern Ist Class Neck Order.

Example as above in the original presentation case.

Form 2, add "f. Medal of Merit (Verdienstmedaille). A 40mm circular enamel medal depicting a red enamel cross with a black enamel eagle with red cross shield on its chest. The reverse bears the inscription on the horizontal bar "Für Verdienste um das Deutsche Rote Kreuze." Finish to the reverse is gold."

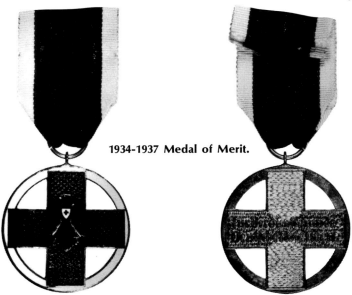

1934-1937 Medal of Merit.

1937-1939 Breast Star to the Grand Cross in its original presentation case showing also the ribbon bar with metal miniature device. The exterior of the case is red, while the interior is blue.

114.

Willy Liebel, Oberburgermeister of Nürnberg, wears the 1937-1939 Pattern 1st Class Neck Order.

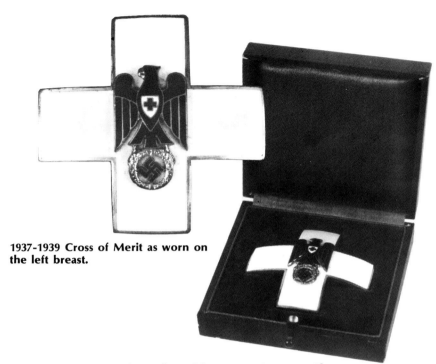

1937-1939 Cross of Merit as worn on the left breast.

As above, but with presentation case. The exterior is red, and the interior blue.

1937-1939 Pattern 2nd Class award as worn on a parade-mount ribbon.

118.

1937-1939 Medal of the German Red Cross. Note that the specimen at the left has no red cross shield on its chest, while the one at the right does.

119

10 Year Sister's Service Cross as worn suspended from a red bow.

Cased 10 Year Sister's Service Cross. The exterior is red, while the interior is blue with silver interior lid designation.

123.

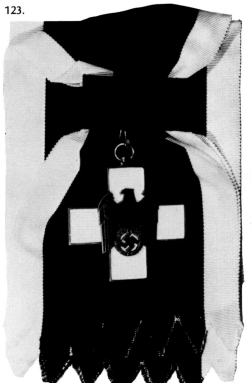

Sash Order with sash badge for the Special Class of the Social Welfare Decoration. The sash ribbon measures 100mm wide.

128.

Presentation case for the 1st Class award. Shown at the base of the blue velvet interior is the red and white lapel ribbon on black button.

130. 3rd Class: ". . . a 35mm red ribbon with white edges. The reverse of the cross was plain gold-colored."

131.

2nd Class pin back badge in its original presentation case.

132.

3rd Class German Social Welfare Decoration.

3rd Class German Social Welfare Decoration with swords and presentation case.

Female version (as worn with the bow) of the 3rd Class.

133.

For some unexplained reason, there exists a bronze version of the Social Welfare Medal. The medal is identical to the silver version, only the finish is in bronze.

141. Add: "The 25 Year award document was signed by Meissner, while the 40 and 50 Year document was signed by Hitler."

154.

Engel

Men's 3rd Class award (12 years) in original presentation box. The box is identical to the four year, but with a "12" stenciled in silver.

Female Four Year Long Service award with original presentation box. The specimen is identical to that of the men's, but the box is wider, and with a shorter length due to the bow suspension.

154.

Men's 25 Year Service award presentation box in blue with gold RAD emblem stenciled on the lid.

167.

Improved photography of the 1936-pattern Fire Brigade decoration 1st Class.

Littlejohn

It appears that a 43mm pinback version was produced. It is possible that this was a transitional piece in brief use prior to the introduction of the gold cross suspended from a ribbon.

172.

Customs award with the emblem embroidered in yellow thread onto the
cornflower blue ribbon. Shown also is
the original presentation box with
green exterior. The interior is buff
color.

178. Line 11: ". . . on the reverse (never raised!)."

End of page: "Erich Koch lost his Golden Party Badge while attending an opera,
and was required to make a request for replacement through official channels.
He was emphatic that the serial number be as originally awarded."

179.

Three examples of the 30.5mm Golden Party Badge. Note that the specimen at the top
has the serial number engraved at the top of the pin rather than below as normally
found. Note also that only one of the three examples has the vent hole (under vertical
pin).

179.

Four examples of the 25mm Golden Party Badge.

182.

Reverse of the Golden Party Badge awarded for outstanding service. Note 25mm specimen at left with lapel bar.

Note the different form (engraved) A.H. initials from those normally encountered.

183. Line 12: "Number 55" to read "Number 555."

186.

Party Leader Dr. Karl Astel wears a Gau Munich Commemorative badge on the lapel of his civilian suit.

190.

SS-Brigadeführer Ulrich Graf, a Party Member since 1920, wears the Blood Order as prescribed by regulations.

Close-up of 2nd Pattern Blood Order (reverse).

191.

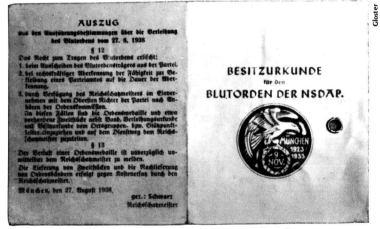

Gloster

Front of the Blood Order Besitzurkunde.

196.

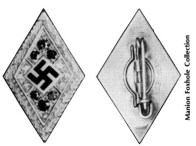

Manion Foxhole Collection

Variation of the Special Class Golden Hitler Youth
Honor Badge. Note that the oakleaf wreath is stamped
flat rather than being raised. The reverse is marked
"M1/128" and RZM logo.

202.

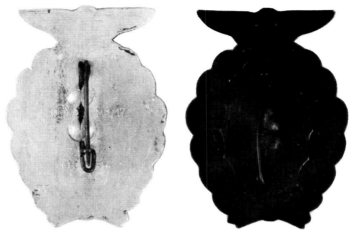

Reverse of the stamped version (right) and the solid version (left). The solid version bears the RZM logo and the mark "M1/17" and below pin "Ges.Gesch."

205. Line 11: "black enamel" to read "black enamel paint."

Obverse of the 1923 version.

210.

Silver version of the East Hanover Gau Commemorative Badge.

397

213. End of paragraph: "A high-quality miniature was produced for this badge . . . normally in the form of a stickpin."

Improved photograph of the Gau Sudetenland Commemorative Badge.

214.

An SS-Obergruppenführer wears the Gau Warthe badge during an inspection tour with Hans Frank on the Eastern Front in 1942.

217.

Miniatures of the 10 Year NSDAP Long Service Medal. At left is the version worn by the women as mounted on a bow (and showing the reverse of the medal), while at right is the standard pattern version as worn by men.

221. End of Paragraph: "There is an example that exists of the 25 Year NSDAP Long Service that is a pin-back badge version rather than the normal medal version."

224. "The Goebbels Diaries" give the date of award of Gauleiter Karl Hanke as 8 April 1945.

226.

Ailsby

Example of the prototype using the Swords version of the Knight's Cross of the Iron Cross. The device was in gold.

Reverse of yet another prototype design of the German Order with Oakleaves and Swords.

227.

Another version of the presentation case of the German Order. The exterior is red, while the lower interior is grey velvet and a white interior lid.

234.

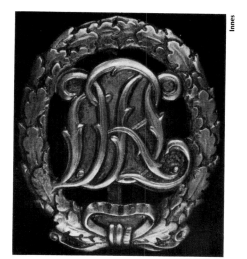

1933 Pattern "DRL" badge with solid letters--a variation of the norm.

237. Line 9: ". . . 'RJA' (Reichs-Jugend-Abzeichen also Reichssports-jugendabzeichen) . . ."

238. Line 6: "A badge was produced with a short bar protruding from the left and right center of the badge. It is presumed that this was the female version."

Line 8: ". . . in bronze only. However, some specimens have been observed in silver."

245. Bottom caption: "There exist cloth versions without any year date."

246. Line 1: Delete sentence "The only . . . silver and gold." Insert "The badge was produced in bronze, silver and gold, but the latter two are seldom encountered."

Line 8: ". . . horizontal pin, and normally bears . . ."

249. End of Para: "A third and final pattern of the DLV Ballonabzeichen took the form of a 22mm round silver stickpin depicting a balloon in blue enamel with silver swastika, and with blue enamel wings protruding from each side of the gondola. The initials "DLV" in blue enamel were also shown. The presentation case was an elongated hinged case with black exterior, white velvet internal base, and white satin interior lid. There was no case designation."

Third pattern DLV Balloonist badge.

**Cased version of the DLV
3rd Pattern stickpin.**

254.   d. Achievement badges "A" (one gull surrounded by an oakleaf wreath); "B" (two gulls and wreath); "C" (three gulls and wreath). The latter was for long range durability flying. This series was referred to as the "Leistungsprüfung (grade)" or Leistungsabzeichen."

Hand-embroidered version of the Achievement A badge. The series also came in enamel lapel pins.

256. Delete photo at center right. Authenticity not verified.

263. "A miniature stickpin version was authorized for wear with the civilian clothes."

265. End of paragraph of German Horse Driver's Badge: "A stickpin miniature was authorized for wear on the civilian clothes."

266.

Hand-embroidered gold on black Young German Horseman's badge.

Kipp

266. End of paragraph at top of page: "Regulations prescribed one class only (bronze), but specimens exist in white metal (aluminum). The wreath is with a leaf pattern."

266. Line 4: ". . . in horsemanship. Other authorized recipients were members of the Wehrmacht, police, NSKK, SS and SA enrolled in riding associations and riding schools."

YOUNG GERMAN HORSE DRIVER'S BADGE
(Deutsches Jugend-Fahrer-Abzeichen)

No information has surfaced on this badge other than existing specimens. The round badge is in bronze and silver with outer leaf pattern and an "R" in a circle at the base. The outer rim of the reverse bears the manufacturer's name and control information.

266.

Obverse and reverse of the German Expert Horseman's Badge in silver.

272. Line 3: "(a) 1000 meter sprint" to read "100 meter sprint."

Golden Leader's Sports Badge with miniature.

(Above) Standard pattern small LDO box that contained the miniature badge. The name "Dr. Fromm" is that of the original recipient.

(Left) Presentation case for the full size badge. The cardboard box has a burgundy exterior color, while the interior base is of burgundy velvet.

277.

Cloth version of the German Youth Proficiency Badge.

282.

Original version of the National Leader's School Breast Insigne.

292. Bottom paragraph, line 2: ". . . worn in pinback form . . ." to read ". . . worn in needle form• . . ."

294. Line 1: "The reverse of the large and small badges bore the . . ."

294.

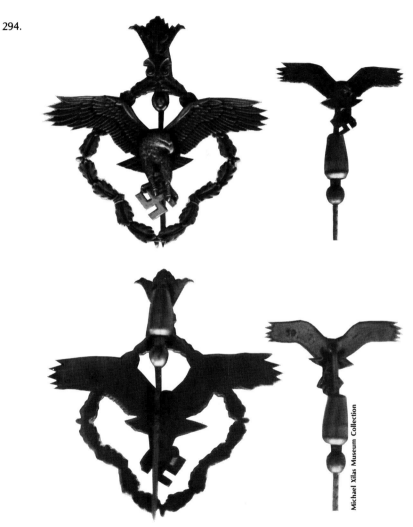

Michael Xilas Museum Collection

Large and small size Commemorative Medal in bronze. Both pieces bear the serial number stamped in the reverse of the award number rendered to the recipient.

Bronze Commemorative Medal in its original presentation case. The exterior is black simulated leather, the base is blue velvet, and the interior lid is white satin. This specimen was presented to Professor Otto Walchner on 1 March 1942. The badge is serial numbered 126.

302. 3rd paragraph, line 3: ". . . gold eagle with black accents surmounting a gold . . ."

303. 3rd paragraph: "The reverse of the badge bore the award serial number near the bottom, and the manufacturer's . . ."

303.

Senate of Culture badge in its original presentation case. The exterior of the case is red, while the lower interior is black velvet, and with a white satin interior lid. There is no lid inscription.

307.

Merit Badges of the NSKOV with white and blue enamel outer border.

310.

Improved photo of the Civil Pilot Badge.

331.

Long and Loyal Service non-portable award for the City of Munich. The award is coin-struck with a high gloss gold finish. The brown simulated leather presentation case has a creme-colored velvet base.

337. End of 2nd paragraph: The awards were rendered by the Reichsverband für Volksmusik (National Association for People's Music).
338. Award presented by "deutscher Sängerbund."

Unidentified unofficial medal (worn about the neck) having to do with some aspect of the NS German Lawyer's Assn. The reverse is marked "GH 900," and is gilt over silver. Neck ribbon is dark blue.

339. Last sentence: "The award takes the form of a stickpin, and was in bronze or silver (silver-grey). A similar badge, but depicting a surface ship, was also produced."

345. Top photo caption: "A miniature version of this badge was also produced."

346.

The political leader at the right wears the Schlageter Bund Commemorative badge. The boy at the right is John Beckwith, later of the British SS Legion.

Bibliography

Brinkman, Jürgen: Orden und Ehrenzeichen des "Dritten Reiches", Private publication, Minden, 1975.

Der Schulungsbrief , 1934-1942.

Doehle, Dr. Heinrich, Orden und Ehrenzeichen im Dritten Reich, Berliner Buch, Berlin, 1939.

Gottgrüsse des ehrfame Handwerk (Honor Book of the German Handworkers), Verlag des neue Deutschland, Leipzig, 1934.

Grunberger, Richard, The 12-Year Reich, Ballentine Books, New York, 1971.

Jahrbuch der Deutschen Adademie der Luftfahrtforschung, 1938-1943.

Klietmann, Dr. Kurt-Gerhard: Deutsche Auszeichnungen - Deutsches Reich 1871-1945, Verlag "Die Ordens-Sammlung", Berlin, 1971.

Klietmann, Dr. Kurt-Gerhard: Selected Monographs.

Littlejohn and Dodkins: Orders, Decorations, Medals and Badges of the Third Reich, Bender Publications, Mountain View, 1968.

Littlejohn and Dodkins: Orders, Decorations, Medals and Badges of the Third Reich, Vol 2, Bender Publications, Mountain View, 1973.

Nationalsozialistischer Lehrerbund/NSLB/Jahrbuch 1935, Fichte Verlag, Munich, 1934.

NSDAP Partei-Statistik, 1935, Vols I-IV, Zentralverlag der NSDAP, 1936.

Riegler, Dr. Hans: Deutscher Luftschutz Jahrbuch, Berlin, 1940.

Rühle, Gerd: Das Dritte Reich, 1936, Vol. IV, Hummelverlag, Berlin, 1937.

Sawicki, James A.: Nazi Decorations and Medals - 1933-1945, published privately, New York, 1958.

Schönleben, Eduard: Fritz Todt, Verlag Gerhard Stalling, Oldenburg, 1943.

Shirer, William L.: The Rise and Fall of the Third Reich, Simon and Schuster, NY, 1960.

Speer, Albert: Inside the Third Reich, Avon Books, NY, 1971.

SS-Dienstaltersliste der Schutzstaffel der NSDAP, Organization list of SS Officer Personnel, 1937 edition.

Uniformen-Markt, Trade paper of the manufacturers, selected editions, 1938-1942.

Verordnungsblatt der SA, Official orders of the SA, 1933-1943

Verordnungsblatt der Waffen-SS, official orders of the Waffen-SS, 1940-1945.

Wykes, Alan: The Nürnberg Rallies, Ballantine Books, Inc., NY, 1970.